The Master Key

A Faculty Guide to Unlocking Student Success in Doctoral Research

Dave Schippers, Sc.D.

Iron Dog LLC

Grand Rapids

Published in the United States by Iron Dog LLC

Dave Schippers.

the master key: a faculty guide to unlocking student success in doctoral research

Includes bibliographical references and index.

ISBN 979-8-9922934-6-3

1. Doctoral dissertation supervision, 2. Dissertation chair leadership, 3. Doctoral mentorship and faculty development, 4. Research design alignment and proposal development, 5. Academic argumentation and scholarly writing, 6. Ethical dissertation supervision and academic integrity, 7. Institutional governance in doctoral education, 8. IRB and ARB compliance in research oversight, 9. Trauma-informed academic mentorship, 10. Neurodiversity and inclusive doctoral supervision, 11. Artificial intelligence in doctoral research and writing, 12. Feedback precision and doctoral performance intervention, 13. Doctoral program quality assurance and policy alignment, 14. Transformational leadership in higher education.

Table of Contents

Editor's Foreword

The Master Key: A Faculty Guide to Unlocking Student Success in Doctoral Research emerges from a bold initiative to redefine not only what doctoral education can be—but what doctoral mentorship must become.

Originally conceived as a supplemental text for evolving doctoral programs, this book was written with a specific goal: to equip faculty with the tools, vision, and courage to lead students through their most challenging academic endeavor— not as evaluators of performance, but as stewards of transformation.

Figure EF.1. Nastrodavus [1].

When the opportunity arose to build a world-class doctoral program at Walsh College, the guiding vision was clear: academic rigor must be matched with intentional design, and scholarly standards must be delivered through mentorship models that are humane, ethical, and effective. Gone are the days when vague expectations and gatekeeping defined doctoral success. In their place, we now call for clarity, structure, and mentorship grounded in psychological safety and professional growth.

As someone who has personally traversed the doctoral landscape—without the benefit of clear guidance—I know the costs of ambiguity. Too many faculty, and too many students, carry the residue of academic trauma masked as tradition. This book is born from the determination to break that cycle. It replaces confusion with process, isolation with mentorship, and institutional delay with actionable momentum.

Just as importantly, this work reflects my commitment to innovation, including the thoughtful use of emerging technologies. *The Master Key* was developed with the aid of generative AI tools—used not to write for us, but to accelerate foundational drafts, allowing more time for deep authorial insight, refinement, and strategic clarity. This fusion of technological capability and human expertise is not an experiment—it is the future of scholarly work, modeled here for faculty leading the next generation.

To every faculty member reading this: know that this text is not merely a how-to manual. It is a manifesto for ethical doctoral leadership. It invites you to reject toxic norms, to confront unconscious academic legacies, and to step into a role that changes lives—not just through content expertise, but through intentional mentorship.

The Master Key is your guide to unlocking potential—not only in your students, but in yourself. Welcome to a new kind of doctoral education. One that transforms not just scholars, but the leaders who shape them.

-Nastrodavus

Author's Foreword

Doctoral programs stand at the pinnacle of academic pursuit, promising mastery in research, critical inquiry, and innovation. Yet they also carry the highest dropout rates of any degree path—a sobering indicator that something within the system is profoundly broken. While the doctoral journey is meant to be transformative, it too often becomes a crucible of confusion, isolation, and academic trauma. Students enter with vision and leave—if they leave at all—exhausted, disillusioned, or worse, silently defeated.

At the heart of this crisis is not simply student attrition, but faculty abdication. The structures of higher education and accreditation, while well-intentioned, have created a culture in which doctoral mentorship has been reduced to gatekeeping, procedural compliance, or passive oversight. The result? An invisible but deeply entrenched message: *"Figure it out on your own."*

The most critical component of doctoral success has never been a database or a policy—it's always been a faculty member willing to mentor with intention. But too often, students find themselves navigating a vast and uncharted sea of expectations, guided only by vague feedback, institutional inertia, or chairs still carrying the scars of their own doctoral wounds.

This is where the cycle must break.

Many faculty—through no fault of their own—inherit and unknowingly perpetuate cultures of delay, hierarchy, and intellectual hazing. Scarred by their own academic trials, they may replicate patterns of non-support, arbitrary gatekeeping, or prolonged silence. It's a kind of academic intergenerational trauma—a legacy of dysfunction passed down in the name of rigor.

The Master Key: A Faculty Guide to Unlocking Student Success in Doctoral Research was written to challenge this culture of dysfunction—and to equip faculty with the tools to build something better.

This book is not simply a procedural manual. It is a call to reclaim doctoral mentorship as a practice of leadership, not endurance. It offers faculty clear strategies for creating structure, giving actionable feedback, supporting diverse learners, and establishing ethical, growth-oriented mentoring relationships. Just as importantly, it names the dysfunction that has long gone unspoken—bias, neglect, ego-driven delays—and invites faculty to lead differently.

Doctoral education should not be a test of survival. It should be a journey of transformation—*for the student and the chair alike*. The role of the faculty mentor is not to replicate the wounds of their past, but to break the cycle and build a more conscious, compassionate, and high-impact model of scholarship.

The Master Key is your invitation to do just that. Not just to supervise dissertations—but to unlock the scholar within every student you serve.

Welcome to the work that changes everything.

How to Use This Book as a Faculty Training Program

This book is not designed to be read once and shelved. It is structured to function as a faculty development sequence—whether for new dissertation chairs, experienced faculty seeking recalibration, or doctoral program leadership teams.

It can be implemented in three primary formats:

1. Individual Chair Development

For individual faculty members:

Figure HTU1. [222].

1. **Begin with Section 1 (Chapters 1–4)**
   Focus on ethical calibration and role clarity.
   Complete all self-assessments honestly.
2. **Move to Section 2 (Chapters 5–11)**
   Study the structural and procedural mechanics of dissertation leadership.
   Use the embedded checklists in real time with active doctoral candidates.
3. **Complete Section 3 (Chapters 12–16)**
   Refine communication, performance intervention, AI-era judgment, and leadership presence.

Recommended approach:

- Read one chapter per week.
- Apply at least one checklist immediately in your current supervision practice.
- Conduct a self-review using the Chair Competency Model at the end of each section.

2. Cohort-Based Faculty Training (8–12 Weeks)

For deans or program directors implementing formal training:

Weeks 1–2:
Chair identity, power, and ethical calibration (Chapters 1–4)

Weeks 3–6:
Research design alignment, proposal readiness, IRB/ARB processes (Chapters 5–10)

Weeks 7–8:
Defense preparation and scholarly argumentation (Chapters 8–11)

Weeks 9–10:
Communication, performance management, and AI supervision (Chapters 12–16)

Each session should include:

- Discussion of one chapter
- Review of one checklist
- Application to a real or simulated case
- Reflection using the competency framework

3. Ongoing Chair Performance Calibration

Programs may use this book as a recurring audit tool:

- Annual chair self-assessment using the Core Competencies
- Checklist-based review before proposal approval
- IRB and ARB readiness verification
- Pre-defense readiness confirmation
- Structured intervention protocol for performance concerns

This converts the book into a governance-aligned quality control system rather than a theoretical reference.

Guiding Principle

This manual is not about adding work. It is about reducing preventable failure.

When used deliberately, it will:

- Decrease redesign cycles
- Reduce attrition
- Improve proposal and defense outcomes
- Clarify institutional expectations
- Elevate doctoral mentorship standards

Use it not as commentary, but as operating procedure.

Section 1: Understanding the Role of a Dissertation Chair

Before you can lead a student through the complexity of a doctoral dissertation, you must first confront the landscape of your own academic formation. Every chair brings a history—of mentors who inspired, processes that frustrated, feedback that wounded, and structures that saved. These personal experiences shape how you show up: the assumptions you hold, the systems you tolerate, and the mentorship you model [1].

Figure S1. [222].

But too often, this inner terrain goes unexamined. We inherit habits of supervision without questioning whether they serve or sabotage. We replicate methods because "that's how it's always been done"—forgetting that doctoral education, at its core, should be about transformation, not tradition [2].

This first section invites you to pause. To turn inward.
Not to critique your students, but to assess your *own readiness* to mentor.

Are you reinforcing the very cycles that once discouraged you?
Are you unintentionally protecting dysfunction under the name of academic rigor?
Have you made peace with your own dissertation journey, or are you still reacting to it?

The chapters ahead will not ask you to be perfect. But they will challenge you to be honest. Because until we examine the ways we were shaped, we cannot reshape the experience for others.

This is where the real work begins—not with templates or timelines, but with the inner reorientation that makes mentorship ethical, conscious, and transformational.

Let's begin—where all journeys of leadership must begin—with the self.

Chapter 1 – Reflecting on Your Doctoral Journey

Figure 1. [222].

The doctoral journey is often described as an odyssey; one marked by intellectual discovery, perseverance, and the relentless pursuit of knowledge [3]. Yet, those who have traveled this path understand that it is not simply an academic exercise; it is a transformation of the self. The journey to a doctorate is demanding, often riddled with moments of uncertainty, imposter syndrome, and the weight of balancing personal and professional obligations. It is a crucible of endurance, shaped not only by rigorous research and scholarship but also by the mentorship, guidance, and academic culture in which it unfolds [4].

For those who have successfully defended their dissertations and earned the title of "Doctor," the question remains: What will you do with the lessons learned from your journey? How will you process your own experiences—both positive and negative—to ensure future doctoral candidates receive the mentorship, support, and guidance they need to succeed? Will you replicate the struggles you endured, perpetuating outdated traditions of academic gatekeeping, or will you redefine doctoral education by fostering an environment of collaboration, innovation, and inclusivity?

This chapter invites you to engage in a critical reflection of your own doctoral experience. Did you receive the mentorship you needed, or did you face challenges that slowed your progress? Were you empowered to develop as a scholar, or were you left to navigate the complexities of research alone? More importantly, have you taken the time to process these experiences to avoid unconsciously reproducing the same struggles for the next generation of doctoral students?

Now, as a faculty mentor, dissertation chair, or academic leader, you have the power to shape a new doctoral experience—one reflecting the best of what academia can offer while breaking the cycles of isolation, rigidity, and unnecessary hardship that too many students have faced [5]. This chapter will explore the realities of doctoral mentorship, the systemic challenges within academic culture, and the role you play in creating an enhanced doctoral journey. It will challenge you to be intentional in your mentorship, ensuring the doctoral candidates under your guidance not only survive their journey but emerge as confident, capable scholars ready to advance knowledge in their fields[6].

Processing the Past: Have You Broken the Cycle?

Every scholar carries with them the imprints of their own academic experiences—some inspiring, others discouraging. For many doctoral candidates, mentorship is the single most influential factor in their success or struggle. A supportive advisor can make the difference between timely completion and prolonged frustration, between scholarly confidence and self-doubt [7]. Conversely, ineffective, indifferent, or toxic mentorship can create unnecessary obstacles that hinder intellectual growth and professional development.

If you encountered setbacks in your doctoral journey due to lack of guidance, unclear expectations, or an unstructured research process, have you taken the time to ensure you are not unconsciously perpetuating those same barriers for your students? Academia has long been characterized by hierarchical traditions that, in some cases, value perseverance over progress, gatekeeping over growth, and exclusivity over accessibility [9, 10]. As a faculty mentor, your responsibility is not merely to uphold academic rigor but to facilitate a research environment challenging and empowering, rather than discouraging and isolating.

Take a moment to reflect:

- **Did you have a mentor who made a positive impact on your research and professional development?** If so, what were the characteristics that made them effective? Are you intentionally modeling those qualities in your own mentorship?

- **Did you experience unnecessary roadblocks during your doctoral process?** Were they the result of outdated policies, unclear communication, or a lack of structured guidance? Were those roadblocks created because your dissertation chair took two years to complete so you could not go faster? How have you adjusted your own approach to avoid repeating those patterns?

- **Were you encouraged to take intellectual risks and develop independent thought, or were you confined to rigid expectations?** How can you create an environment where doctoral candidates feel safe to explore, innovate, and challenge assumptions?

Understanding your own experience is the first step toward shaping a more effective and empowering doctoral mentorship model.

Creating an Enhanced Doctoral Experience: Your Role as a Mentor and Leader

As a faculty mentor, you now have the opportunity—and the responsibility—to redefine the doctoral experience for the students under your guidance. This role extends beyond simply advising on research methodology or approving dissertation chapters. You are now a facilitator of scholarly growth, a mentor in professional development, and an advocate for student success. Your approach to mentorship will directly impact whether a student thrives in their doctoral journey or becomes another case of academic attrition [11].

A **new model of doctoral mentorship** is emerging, one prioritizing structure, support, and strategic guidance. Key elements of this model include:

- **Intentional Mentorship:** Move beyond the traditional hands-off approach where students are left to "figure it out" on their own. Instead, adopt a mentorship model that includes clear expectations, structured check-ins, and constructive feedback that nurtures both research progress and professional confidence.

- **Modern Research Tools and Methods:** The academic landscape is evolving, and so should the way we mentor doctoral candidates. Encourage the ethical use of generative AI tools, advanced research methodologies, and digital collaboration platforms to streamline research and expand knowledge access. Emphasize efficiency without compromising rigor.

- **Well-Defined Pathways to Success:** Too often, doctoral students face unclear requirements, shifting expectations, and inconsistent feedback [12]. As a mentor, your role is to provide a well-mapped dissertation process, ensuring students understand every stage of their research journey. This includes timelines, milestone tracking, and transparent evaluation criteria.

- **Building a Culture of Collaboration:** The best scholars do not emerge in isolation. Encourage students to engage in **peer review, interdisciplinary research discussions, and collaborative publishing opportunities.** Foster a community where doctoral candidates learn from each other, rather than struggling alone.

- **A Commitment to Student Well-Being:** Doctoral education should challenge, not break, students. Be mindful of the mental health challenges, burnout risks, and work-life balance struggles that many candidates face. Model a culture of academic rigor that is balanced with support, encouragement, and realistic expectations [13].

A Call to Action: Be the Mentor You Wish You Had

Doctoral education is at a crossroads. The next generation of scholars will either inherit the same struggles their mentors faced or benefit from a reimagined, intentional approach to doctoral mentorship that prioritizes excellence without unnecessary hardship. Which model will you contribute to?

Your legacy as a mentor will not be measured solely by how many dissertations you approve but by how many scholars you empower, how many minds you inspire, and how many barriers you help dismantle. The doctoral students you guide today will become the thought leaders, researchers, and educators of tomorrow. Their success is, in part, a reflection of the mentorship they receive.

So ask yourself: Are you perpetuating the old cycle, or are you shaping the new model? Are you mentoring students as you were mentored, or as you wish you had been mentored? Will the doctoral candidates you guide struggle unnecessarily, or will they be equipped with the best tools, the best mentorship, and the best academic experience to reach their full potential?

As you move forward, consider your role in shaping the future of doctoral education. Your students are watching, learning, and carrying your influence with them. The time to redefine the doctoral experience—for them, and for the generations to follow—is now.

Understanding and Reflecting on Doctoral Journey Transformation

The doctoral journey is often described as a transformative experience—one reshaping not only a candidate's intellectual abilities but also their self-perception, resilience, and professional identity [14]. However, this transformation is not solely about academic growth; it also involves navigating complex interpersonal relationships, institutional dynamics, and deeply ingrained systemic challenges.

One of the most overlooked aspects of this journey is the influence of mentorship—both its positive potential and its potential to create negative cycles that hinder student success.

Breaking the Negative Cycles of Doctoral Mentorship

While mentorship is a cornerstone of doctoral education, it is not always effective or equitable. Many students encounter obstacles arising not from the research process itself but from the very structures meant to support them. These challenges can manifest in various forms, including strained relationships with advisors, implicit or explicit biases, and imbalances of power within academia. By recognizing and addressing these issues, both students and faculty can work toward a healthier, more constructive mentoring environment.

People Problems: Navigating Interpersonal Challenges in Doctoral Mentorship

One of the most common barriers to a positive doctoral experience is conflict within mentoring relationships. Doctoral students rely heavily on their advisors and committee members for guidance, yet these relationships can become strained due to mismatched expectations, poor communication, or personality clashes [15]. Some common challenges include:

- **Lack of Clear Guidance:** Some advisors adopt a hands-off approach, leaving students to navigate complex research and administrative requirements without sufficient support [16]. This can lead to confusion, stagnation, and frustration.

- **Overbearing Supervision:** Conversely, some mentors exert excessive control over their students' research, limiting intellectual freedom and discouraging independent thought [17].

- **Unrealistic Expectations:** Students may struggle under the weight of demanding expectations that do not account for personal circumstances, mental health, or work-life balance.

To break these negative cycles, students must be empowered to advocate for themselves, set clear boundaries, and seek support from institutional resources when needed. Meanwhile, faculty members should receive training in effective mentorship, emphasizing the importance of adaptability, empathy, and constructive feedback.

Confronting Prejudice: Addressing Bias in Doctoral Mentorship

Bias—whether conscious or unconscious—remains an issue in doctoral education [18]. Prejudice can manifest in various ways, from gender and racial discrimination to biases based on research interests, methodologies, or career aspirations. These biases can affect funding opportunities, publication prospects, and even a student's ability to complete their dissertation successfully.

For instance, students from underrepresented backgrounds may encounter additional scrutiny or be expected to "prove themselves" more than their peers [19]. Some may struggle to find mentors who understand their experiences, leading to feelings of isolation and discouragement. Others may face microaggressions, subtle yet harmful comments that undermine confidence and belonging.

Confronting these issues requires institutional commitment to diversity, equity, and inclusion. Universities must actively promote mentorship programs that prioritize diversity, provide training to faculty on recognizing and mitigating bias, and create safe spaces where students can voice concerns without fear of retaliation [20]. At the individual level, both students and mentors should cultivate awareness of their own biases and strive to foster inclusive, supportive academic environments.

Power: Challenging Hierarchies in Doctoral Education

The academic system is deeply hierarchical, with power concentrated among faculty, administrators, and senior researchers [21]. Doctoral students, often seen as apprentices rather than emerging scholars, may feel powerless when facing conflicts with advisors or institutional policies [22]. This power imbalance can discourage students from advocating for themselves, leading to prolonged program timelines, research exploitation, or even attrition [23].

Power dynamics also influence who gets credit for research contributions, whose work is prioritized for funding, and whose voices are amplified in academic discourse. Some students find themselves working on projects dictated entirely by their advisors, with little room to explore their own research interests. Others may hesitate to challenge feedback or request changes to their committee, fearing retaliation or stalled progress [25, 28].

Addressing these power imbalances requires a shift in academic culture—one that values doctoral students as colleagues rather than subordinates. Faculty should encourage open dialogue, respect students' autonomy in shaping their research, and recognize their contributions fairly. Additionally, institutions should implement transparent grievance processes that allow students to report issues without jeopardizing their academic careers.

Final Reflections

Breaking the negative cycles of doctoral mentorship is not just about improving individual experiences—it is about transforming academia into a more equitable, supportive, and intellectually enriching environment. By addressing interpersonal conflicts, confronting prejudice, and challenging power imbalances, doctoral students can reclaim their agency, and faculty can fulfill their role as true mentors and allies. Reflection on these challenges is the first step toward meaningful change, ensuring that future generations of scholars enter an academic world that values not only their intellect but also their well-being.

Honor Your Transition, but Break Any Negative Cycles

The journey to earning a doctorate is transformative, demanding, and deeply personal. It marks a transition from student to scholar, from knowledge consumer to knowledge creator. However, while this transition should be celebrated as an achievement, it is equally important to recognize and address the negative cycles within doctoral education that can undermine student success.

Unfortunately, some aspects of academic culture foster toxicity rather than growth. Negative behaviors—whether subtle or overt—can create an environment where students struggle not because of academic challenges, but due to unnecessary and harmful barriers. These behaviors not only hinder research progress but can also take a serious toll on mental health, leading to anxiety, depression, and in some cases, attrition.

Breaking these cycles requires active reflection, self-advocacy, and institutional reform. Doctoral students must be empowered to recognize when they are in unhealthy situations, seek support, and challenge practices that perpetuate harm. At the same time, faculty and administrators must take responsibility for fostering a culture of respect, inclusion, and constructive mentorship.

Examples of Toxic Behavior in Doctoral Education

Toxic behaviors in doctoral education can take many forms, some overt and others more insidious. Recognizing these patterns is the first step toward breaking them.

Verbal Abuse

Harsh, demeaning, or excessively critical language from advisors, faculty, or peers can have lasting effects on a student's confidence and well-being. While constructive criticism is essential for academic growth, verbal abuse crosses the line into harmful territory when it becomes personal, dismissive, or humiliating. Students subjected to verbal abuse often internalize feelings of inadequacy, which can lead to self-doubt, reluctance to seek feedback, or even fear of engaging in academic discussions.

Exclusion

Isolation—whether intentional or unintentional—can be devastating for doctoral students. Some students are left out of research opportunities, professional development events, or even informal networking within their department. Exclusion can take many forms, such as:

- Withholding invitations to important academic meetings
- Ignoring a student's contributions in discussions
- Creating an "in-group" dynamic where certain students receive preferential treatment

Exclusion prevents students from building essential professional connections and accessing critical resources for success, reinforcing feelings of imposter syndrome and marginalization.

Belittling

Dismissing a student's ideas, research interests, or career aspirations as unimportant or unrealistic can be incredibly damaging. Some students experience belittling through:

- Having their research questions ridiculed or deemed "unworthy" of academic pursuit
- Being told their work is not as rigorous or valuable as traditional research paths
- Experiencing condescending treatment that undermines their contributions

Belittling stifles creativity, discourages independent thought, and erodes the self-confidence necessary for scholarly success.

Discrimination

Systemic and individual biases continue to shape doctoral education. Discrimination based on race, gender, age, disability, sexual orientation, socioeconomic status, or research interests can create significant barriers to academic achievement. Discriminatory practices include:

- Unequal access to funding or research opportunities

- Biased feedback that favors certain groups over others

- Institutional policies that disproportionately impact marginalized students

Many students from underrepresented backgrounds experience additional scrutiny or skepticism about their academic capabilities, making it even more challenging to thrive in doctoral programs [24].

When Rigor Becomes Harm: Toxic Behavior in Doctoral Culture

Toxicity in doctoral education is not always overt. It often hides beneath the surface of tradition, masquerading as rigor, objectivity, or "what we all went through." [26] But for many students—especially first-generation scholars and those navigating mental health challenges—these covert patterns are not just discouraging. They are demoralizing. Below are common, yet deeply harmful, examples of toxic behavior that faculty may unwittingly perpetuate.

Aggression Toward First-Generation Doctoral Students

"You're not quite ready for this level of work."

Vignette:
Maria, the first in her family to finish high school, worked two jobs while completing her master's degree. In her first dissertation planning meeting, her chair comments, "You're passionate, but I'm not sure you have the academic polish we're looking for." No specifics. No path forward. Just a gate slammed shut. Maria leaves the meeting questioning whether her background, not her work, is being judged—and she's right.

Reflection:
Such statements are rarely about actual capability. They often reflect faculty discomfort with unfamiliar narratives of success. When a student's cultural capital doesn't match the expected mold—e.g., prestigious undergrad, parental support, scholarly lineage—it's all too easy to question their legitimacy. This is not mentorship. It's gatekeeping disguised as guidance [27].

Dismissal of Mental Health Disclosures

"Doctoral work is supposed to be stressful."

Vignette:
Jalen, a doctoral student with generalized anxiety disorder, discloses to his committee that he's been struggling with panic attacks during the IRB delay and looming deadlines. His chair sighs and replies, "Look, we've all been there. This is part of the process. If you can't handle pressure, maybe this isn't the right path."

Reflection:
This is not tough love—it's psychological harm. Equating mental illness with weakness sends a chilling message: *only the silent and suffering are worthy of doctoral success*. Faculty who dismiss disclosures like these not only risk exacerbating student distress—they also model a toxic definition of academic excellence rooted in stoicism, not strength [29].

Other Toxic Phrases and Patterns to Watch For:

- "We only take serious students here." (As if disclosure = unseriousness)
- "This isn't therapy—it's academia." (False binary. Students are whole people.)
- "No one held my hand when I did this." (Rite-of-passage mentality weaponized)
- "That's just how this committee operates." (Normalization of dysfunction)

Reframing the Role of the Chair

Toxicity thrives in silence and tradition. Your role as a chair is not to reinforce the harshness you endured—it's to consciously interrupt harm, name it, and replace it with courageous compassion. That doesn't mean lowering standards. It means expanding the definition of scholarly worth and remembering that behind every dissertation draft is a human life in motion.

Ask yourself:

- Would you say this to a peer?
- Would you want your own child or mentee treated this way?
- Have you mistaken discomfort with deficiency?

Leadership in doctoral education begins when we replace elitism with empathy—and when we realize that survival should not be the benchmark of success [30].

Unseen Minds: Neurodiversity and the Myth of the "Ideal" Doctoral Student

In the shadow of traditional academic mentorship lies a silent but persistent bias—one that favors linearity, conformity, and neurotypicality. The archetype of the "ideal" doctoral student is often unspoken but deeply ingrained: focused, hyper-organized, emotionally regulated, and capable of managing stress without visible struggle. This image, though convenient for faculty expectations, excludes a significant—and growing—portion of doctoral candidates: those who are neurodivergent, have non-linear academic paths, or live with trauma-impacted cognition such as PTSD [18].

If we do not consciously break this cognitive conformity bias, we risk marginalizing students who are no less brilliant—but whose minds work differently.

Consider the student with ADHD, whose intellect is vast but whose executive functioning can falter under ambiguous instructions or delayed feedback. Left unsupported, they may internalize failure not as a structural mismatch, but as a personal flaw. Or the candidate on the autism spectrum, who interprets feedback literally, struggles with unwritten academic expectations, and is often misunderstood in committee meetings as "rigid" or "uncoachable" when, in fact, they are seeking clarity—not conflict. Or the first-generation veteran with undiagnosed PTSD, who struggles to sit through a three-hour dissertation defense preparation because hypervigilance and somatic tension make stillness feel like a threat [19].

These are not exceptions. These are your students.

Yet many of our current mentorship practices unintentionally compound their challenges:

- Ambiguity in expectations becomes a trap, not a challenge.
- Slow or vague feedback erodes motivation and exacerbates shame spirals.
- Hyperfocus on deadlines over development alienates students whose processing is nonlinear but no less rigorous [20].

To break this cycle, we must begin by shattering the myth of the one-size-fits-all doctoral path. True academic rigor is not compromised by flexibility; it is revealed by it. Providing neurodivergent students with scaffolded feedback, predictable structures, and space to process in their own tempo is not accommodation—it is intellectual inclusion. And it benefits all students, not just those with diagnoses [20].

Ask yourself:

- Are your expectations equitable—or simply familiar?
- Have you created room for brilliance that looks different than your own?
- Do you see your mentees clearly—or only the ones who mirror your academic persona?

To mentor in the modern era is not just to teach—it is to deconstruct the invisible curriculum of doctoral success and rebuild it to include every kind of mind.

This is your opportunity to be not just a gatekeeper of knowledge, but a liberator of potential.

Refusing Students Who Are ESL – A Frequently Abused Bias

One of the most troubling forms of discrimination is the rejection or mistreatment of students who speak English as a second language (ESL) [21]. While strong academic writing is essential, using language proficiency as a gatekeeping mechanism—rather than providing adequate support—is an abuse of power. This often manifests as:

- Denying opportunities or funding based on perceived writing difficulties

- Excessively harsh grading or feedback that disregards content in favor of grammar perfection

- Dismissing valuable research because of linguistic biases [22]

Rather than setting students up for failure, institutions should provide writing resources, mentorship, and constructive feedback to help ESL students succeed. Academic excellence is not defined solely by linguistic perfection, but by the depth and rigor of intellectual contributions.

Setting Up Students for Termination

Some faculty members intentionally or unintentionally create environments where students are set up to fail [23]. This can happen through:

- Withholding necessary guidance on dissertation progress

- Refusing to provide clear expectations or milestones

- Assigning unrealistic workloads that make timely completion impossible

When students are placed in a situation where success is unattainable, the emotional toll can be severe. Many doctoral candidates who face these conditions end up leaving their programs, often blaming themselves rather than recognizing systemic failures [24].

Giving Students "Unsatisfactory" Ratings Without Justification

Subjective and unfair evaluations are another method used to gatekeep doctoral success. Some students receive negative performance reviews or unsatisfactory dissertation feedback without clear reasoning or actionable suggestions for improvement [25]. This lack of transparency:

- Creates confusion and frustration

- Leaves students without a path forward

- Undermines trust in the mentoring relationship

Faculty should be required to provide concrete feedback, clear improvement plans, and measurable expectations rather than using vague or arbitrary ratings to push students out of the program [26].

Breaking the Cycle: A Call for Change

To honor the transition into scholarly life, doctoral students must be supported—not broken down. This requires a commitment from both students and faculty to challenge toxic behaviors, advocate for fair treatment, and foster an environment that prioritizes academic and personal well-being.

- **For Students:** Recognize when toxic behaviors are present, seek support from trusted mentors, and utilize institutional resources for conflict resolution.

- **For Faculty:** Actively work to create a supportive research culture, provide clear and constructive feedback, and advocate for inclusive mentorship practices.

- **For Institutions:** Implement policies that protect students from discrimination, ensure fair evaluation processes, and hold faculty accountable for toxic behaviors.

The doctoral journey should be challenging in an intellectual sense, but it should not be needlessly destructive. By acknowledging and breaking these negative cycles, we can build a more ethical, supportive, and empowering academic community for future scholars.

Self-Assessment Introduction: Confronting the Mentorship You Model

Before you can lead doctoral candidates toward intellectual independence, you must confront an uncomfortable possibility: you may be reproducing the very conditions that once made your own journey harder than it needed to be.

Doctoral mentorship is rarely neutral. Every delay, every comment, every silence communicates a philosophy of scholarship. Students are not only learning research design, argumentation, and methodological rigor from you—they are learning what power looks like, what leadership feels like, and what kind of academic culture they will eventually replicate.

Too often, faculty inherit mentorship habits unexamined. We normalize prolonged feedback cycles as "rigor." We rationalize emotional distance as "professionalism." We confuse ambiguity with intellectual growth. We elevate endurance over development. And in doing so, we silently encode a belief that suffering is a prerequisite for scholarly legitimacy.

The danger is not overt cruelty. It is unconscious replication.

If your doctoral experience was marked by delayed feedback, shifting expectations, intellectual gatekeeping, or emotional detachment, you may believe those hardships built resilience. Perhaps they did. But resilience forged in dysfunction does not justify perpetuating dysfunction. Strength gained through unnecessary hardship does not obligate you to impose it on others.

Doctoral education should be demanding. It should not be destabilizing.

The following self-assessment is not designed to shame you. It is designed to interrupt autopilot. It asks whether your behaviors—intentional or not—are reinforcing a model of mentorship rooted in scarcity, hierarchy, and endurance rather than clarity, structure, and ethical leadership.

Read each item slowly. Resist defensiveness. If even one statement reflects your practice, pause. That pause is the beginning of reform.

Because the question is not whether you survived your doctorate.

The question is whether your students must survive you.

Self-Assessment: Are You Replicating Negative Environment?
Answer honestly:

☐ Do you delay feedback because "they need to learn patience"?

☐ Do you withhold praise because "they shouldn't need validation"?

☐ Do you give vague feedback because "figuring it out builds character"?

☐ Do you increase requirements because "I had to do more"?

☐ Do you avoid difficult conversations because "doctoral students should be self-directed"?

☐ Do you measure success by attrition ("only the strong survive")?

☐ Do you view student mental health concerns as "weakness"?

If you checked ANY box, you are perpetuating doctoral trauma.

Chapter 2 - Introduction to Dissertation Chair Responsibilities

Doctoral research is both a personal odyssey and an intellectual undertaking of the highest order. At its core, it is a rigorous exercise in inquiry, synthesis, and contribution to knowledge. Yet, behind every successful dissertation stands a guiding force—an academic shepherd, a rigorous critic, a tireless motivator—the dissertation chair. As the linchpin of doctoral mentorship, the chair's role is more than supervisory; it is foundational, serving as both the bedrock and scaffolding upon which a student's research aspirations are built.

Figure 2. [222].

A dissertation is not merely a document; it is an evolving conversation between ideas, methodologies, and disciplinary discourses. For doctoral candidates, this process can be overwhelming, marked by uncertainty, self-doubt, and the pressures of scholarly rigor. It is the dissertation chair who transforms this journey from a solitary struggle into a structured, guided expedition. By serving as both mentor and gatekeeper, the chair ensures that the research remains grounded in methodological soundness, theoretical alignment, and academic integrity. However, this mentorship extends beyond research mechanics—it is the cultivation of a scholar's intellectual autonomy, critical thinking, and professional identity.

Effective dissertation chairs do not merely oversee the completion of a dissertation; they cultivate the scholar within. They foster an environment of inquiry and academic resilience, equipping students with the tools necessary to engage in independent research long after their doctoral studies conclude. Their role is not simply to advise but to inspire—to ignite curiosity, to challenge assumptions, and to refine raw ideas into polished scholarship. By nurturing research competence and ethical rigor, they shape the next generation of academics, researchers, and thought leaders.

The Dissertation Chair as a Bridge Between Structure and Independence

One of the most intricate challenges of doctoral mentorship lies in balancing structure with autonomy. The very essence of doctoral research is to develop students into independent scholars capable of conducting original research without excessive reliance on external guidance [27]. However, without direction, even the most promising research ideas can become unfocused, methodologically flawed, or stalled by indecision. The dissertation chair, therefore, must act as both an anchor and a catalyst—providing clear milestones and expectations while fostering independent thinking and intellectual risk-taking.

This balance requires a tailored mentorship approach. No two doctoral students are alike; some thrive with structured timelines and explicit feedback, while others require room to explore ideas through iteration and discovery. The chair's role is to recognize these distinctions and adapt accordingly, guiding each student toward self-sufficiency. This mentorship is dynamic rather than prescriptive, allowing students to navigate their own intellectual landscapes while ensuring that their research meets the highest standards of academic rigor.

Moreover, the dissertation chair must navigate the nuanced dynamics of the dissertation committee. As the primary liaison between the student and the committee members, the chair ensures that feedback remains constructive, expectations remain aligned, and academic debates remain centered on strengthening the dissertation rather than fracturing the research process [28]. Diplomatic coordination is essential in managing conflicting viewpoints, ensuring that committee discussions enhance rather than hinder student progress.

Beyond the Dissertation: The Chair's Role in Professional Development

While the dissertation itself is the focal point of doctoral training, the broader goal of a doctoral program is to prepare scholars for a lifetime of academic and professional contribution. Here, the dissertation chair serves not only as a research mentor but as a career guide, introducing students to the unwritten rules of academia—publishing research, presenting at conferences, and engaging in scholarly discourse.

Encouraging students to publish their findings in reputable academic journals, present their research at conferences, and network with scholars in their field is an essential function of dissertation mentorship. Chairs must guide students in navigating the complexities of peer review, revising manuscripts, and strategically positioning their research for maximum scholarly impact [29]. This process transforms dissertation research from a singular academic requirement into a meaningful contribution to the discipline.

Beyond academia, dissertation chairs also play a pivotal role in preparing students for research-based careers in industry, government, and non-academic organizations [30]. For those pursuing careers outside of traditional faculty roles, chairs must help students articulate the broader implications of their research, highlighting its relevance to policy, business, or technology. In this way, the dissertation chair bridges the gap between academic scholarship and real-world application, ensuring that doctoral research extends beyond the confines of the university and contributes to broader societal advancements.

Conclusion: The Chair as the Master Key

A dissertation chair is more than an advisor; they are a master key—unlocking potential, refining inquiry, and shaping the trajectory of a scholar's intellectual and professional life. The role requires academic expertise, interpersonal finesse, and an unwavering commitment to student success. It demands patience, adaptability, and a profound understanding of both research and human motivation.

The chapters that follow will explore the multifaceted responsibilities of dissertation chairs, from guiding research design and fostering academic integrity to preparing students for the dissertation defense and professional publication. Whether mentoring a first-time researcher or supporting a seasoned professional returning for a terminal degree, the principles outlined in this guide will equip dissertation chairs with the strategies necessary to cultivate excellence in doctoral research.

In the grand symphony of academia, where knowledge is continuously refined and expanded, the dissertation chair is both the conductor and the compass—a guiding force that ensures each student's research journey is marked not only by completion but by transformation.

The Significance of Faculty Mentorship in Doctoral Research

The dissertation chair plays a critical role in the doctoral research process, serving as both a mentor and an academic guide for students as they navigate the complexities of scholarly inquiry. Faculty mentorship extends beyond merely overseeing research—it is an intricate, dynamic relationship that shapes the intellectual and professional development of doctoral candidates [31]. A skilled dissertation chair not only provides guidance on research methodology and theoretical frameworks but also fosters intellectual curiosity, critical thinking, and scholarly independence [32].

Effective mentorship requires a delicate balance between support and challenge, ensuring that students are encouraged to push their academic boundaries while still maintaining a structured pathway toward dissertation completion [33]. A dissertation chair must cultivate an environment where students feel empowered to develop original research contributions while also adhering to rigorous academic standards. Beyond the research process, mentorship also involves professional development, such as guiding students on scholarly publishing, presenting at conferences, and preparing for careers in academia or industry [34].

Furthermore, mentorship in doctoral research is a long-term commitment that requires active engagement, clear communication, and adaptability to each student's individual needs. The ability to recognize and respond to students' evolving research trajectories is fundamental to their academic success. Dissertation chairs who embody strong mentorship principles not only enhance the student's dissertation experience but also contribute to a broader culture of academic excellence and scholarly integrity [35].

Key Responsibilities and Expectations

The role of a dissertation chair encompasses a wide range of responsibilities that extend from initial topic selection to the final dissertation defense. At the core of this role is the responsibility to ensure that doctoral candidates produce original, high-quality research that meets institutional and disciplinary standards [36]. The key responsibilities of a dissertation chair include:

1. Guiding Research Design and Methodology – Dissertation chairs assist students in refining their research questions, selecting appropriate methodologies, and ensuring methodological rigor. This involves providing feedback on research proposals, helping students navigate data collection and analysis, and addressing potential ethical considerations.

2. Providing Constructive Feedback – One of the chair's primary duties is to offer timely, detailed, and constructive feedback on dissertation drafts. Effective feedback should be specific, actionable, and aimed at strengthening both the clarity and scholarly contribution of the research.

3. Facilitating Committee Collaboration – The dissertation chair acts as a liaison between the student and the dissertation committee, ensuring that all members are aligned on expectations

and timelines. This requires diplomatic coordination to address any conflicts or differing perspectives that may arise among committee members.

4. Monitoring Progress and Accountability – Chairs must establish clear milestones and expectations for dissertation completion, helping students remain on track while also adapting timelines to accommodate unforeseen challenges [36]. Regular progress meetings, written progress reports, and structured check-ins can help maintain momentum throughout the research process.

5. Supporting Professional Development – Beyond the dissertation itself, chairs should encourage students to engage in scholarly activities such as publishing their research, presenting at conferences, and networking with other scholars in their field. Professional development mentorship prepares students for future careers in academia, research, or industry.

6. Ensuring Institutional and Ethical Compliance – Dissertation chairs must ensure that research adheres to ethical guidelines, including Institutional Review Board (IRB) approvals, data integrity, and proper citation practices. Upholding these standards protects both the student and the institution's academic credibility [38].

By fulfilling these responsibilities, dissertation chairs play an indispensable role in shaping students' academic journeys, fostering an environment where rigorous inquiry and intellectual growth thrive.

Balancing Student Autonomy with Faculty Guidance

One of the most challenging aspects of dissertation mentorship is striking the right balance between student autonomy and faculty guidance. Doctoral research is intended to be an independent endeavor that showcases the student's ability to conduct original research, but it also necessitates structured support and expert direction from the dissertation chair [39].

Encouraging student autonomy requires fostering an environment where students take ownership of their research while also feeling supported throughout the process. Chairs can promote autonomy by:

- Encouraging students to take the lead in setting research goals and timelines.

- Prompting students to articulate their own interpretations and justifications for their methodological choices.

- Providing opportunities for independent problem-solving before offering direct solutions.

- Reinforcing the importance of self-directed learning, critical thinking, and scholarly resilience.

However, while autonomy is crucial, there are instances where direct guidance is necessary to prevent students from veering off course. Dissertation chairs should intervene when students encounter methodological pitfalls, struggle with coherence in their arguments, or face challenges in synthesizing literature effectively. The goal is not to impose a singular research path but to equip students with the analytical tools and academic discipline needed to refine their own scholarly approach.

Successful dissertation chairs approach this balance through adaptive mentorship, where the level of guidance evolves based on the student's progress and capabilities [40]. Early in the research process, more hands-on support may be required, whereas later stages should involve greater student independence. Striking this balance ensures that doctoral candidates develop the confidence, expertise, and scholarly identity necessary to contribute meaningfully to their fields.

Conclusion

The dissertation chair serves as both a mentor and an academic leader, guiding students through the demanding yet rewarding process of doctoral research. Effective dissertation leadership requires a comprehensive understanding of mentorship, a commitment to structured yet flexible support, and a focus on balancing guidance with student autonomy. By embracing these responsibilities with clarity and purpose, dissertation chairs can unlock the full potential of their students, fostering an environment where research excellence and scholarly innovation can thrive.

The Chair's Mirror: A Pre-Action Integrity Check

Before you send the email. Before you return the draft. Before you add another requirement. Before you stay silent. Pause.

The role of dissertation chair carries authority—structural authority, intellectual authority, and psychological authority. Every decision you make shapes not only a document, but a developing scholar. In that space of influence, your motivations matter as much as your expertise.

Rigor is essential in doctoral education. But rigor without self-awareness becomes rigidity. Standards without reflection become control. Expectations without transparency become punishment disguised as professionalism.

The greatest threat to ethical mentorship is not incompetence. It is unexamined inheritance.

Many chairs do not consciously intend to replicate harm. Yet subtle reenactments occur:

- A delay justified as "teaching independence."

- A harsh tone rationalized as "academic toughness."

- An added hurdle framed as "maintaining standards."

- Silence defended as "self-directed learning."

These decisions often originate not in student need, but in unresolved memory—of how we were treated, how we coped, what we endured.

Doctoral leadership demands more than intellectual mastery. It demands psychological maturity.

The following checklist is not about procedural compliance. It is about ethical calibration. It is a moment of internal audit before exercising power. It asks whether your next move is grounded in student development—or in the reenactment of your own history.

If Chapter 1 asked you to confront inherited patterns, Chapter 2 asks you to interrupt them in real time.

Use this checklist before action, not after regret.

Self-Assessment: Student Interaction Integrity Review

Answer honestly:

□ Am I about to do something my advisor did to me?

□ Am I using "rigor" to justify behavior that's actually punitive?

□ Am I delaying something because I'm avoiding discomfort?

□ Am I making this harder than it needs to be to prove something?

□ Would I treat a colleague this way, or only a student?

□ Am I solving the student's problem or re-enacting my own?

The First 30 Days: Activating Effective Chair Leadership

The tone of a dissertation journey is set immediately.

Not at the proposal defense.
Not during Chapter 3 revisions.
Not when problems emerge.

It is set in the first 30 days.

When a student is assigned to you, they are evaluating more than your credentials. They are assessing your responsiveness, your clarity, your structure, and your leadership. Early ambiguity creates anxiety. Early silence creates doubt. Early disorganization creates momentum loss that can take months to recover.

Doctoral candidates do not fail primarily because they lack intelligence. They struggle because expectations are unclear, timelines are undefined, feedback norms are unstated, and committee coordination is left to chance.

Strong chairs do not allow drift.

The initial phase of supervision is not administrative housekeeping—it is strategic architecture. In these early interactions, you establish:

- Communication norms

- Accountability rhythms

- Milestone visibility

- Committee alignment

- Professional tone

If you do this deliberately, you reduce conflict, accelerate progress, and create psychological safety without lowering standards.

The following checklists operationalize that responsibility. They move mentorship from philosophical intention to structured execution. They ensure that within the first month:

- The student knows how this relationship works.
- The committee knows how this process will move.
- You know the system is stable.

Leadership at the doctoral level is not reactive. It is anticipatory.

This is where you demonstrate that.

Student Dissertation Onboarding Checklist

☐ Schedule initial meeting within 48 hours of assignment

☐ Establish preferred communication channels and response windows

☐ Set recurring check-in schedule (weekly/biweekly/monthly)

☐ Clarify revision turnaround expectations (both directions)

☐ Discuss learning style and feedback preferences

☐ Establish milestone tracking system

☐ Share dissertation timeline template

Committee Coordination Checklist

☐ Introduce yourself to committee members

☐ Clarify committee member expectations and deadlines

☐ Establish committee communication protocol

☐ Schedule proposal review meeting

☐ Confirm defense scheduling procedures

Chapter 3 - Academic and Institutional Guidelines

The journey of doctoral research is not simply a test of intellectual rigor—it is also an intricate navigation of institutional policies, academic expectations, and regulatory frameworks. While the dissertation chair serves as the guiding mentor, empowering students with the tools to conduct original and meaningful research, they must also ensure that this research adheres to the rigorous academic and institutional guidelines that define doctoral scholarship. These guidelines, though often seen as administrative constraints, are in fact the scaffolding that upholds the credibility, integrity, and scholarly merit of doctoral work.

From the first moment a doctoral student conceptualizes their research topic to the triumphant defense of their dissertation, every step is shaped by academic policies, procedural requirements, and ethical considerations. Universities, accreditation bodies, and academic review boards establish these structures to maintain the highest scholarly standards while safeguarding the rights of researchers, participants, and the broader academic community [41]. The dissertation chair, therefore, must be both a mentor and a steward of institutional compliance, ensuring that students meet these expectations without stifling their intellectual independence.

Figure 3. [222].

This chapter serves as a roadmap for dissertation chairs, detailing the essential academic and institutional guidelines that govern doctoral research. By mastering these frameworks, chairs can proactively guide students through the complexities of proposal approvals, formatting requirements, ethical research standards, and dissertation committee coordination. The goal is not to impose bureaucratic hurdles but to integrate these academic guardrails seamlessly into the research process, allowing students to thrive within the structure rather than feeling constrained by it.

Understanding University Dissertation Policies

A dissertation chair must possess a deep and comprehensive understanding of university dissertation policies to effectively guide doctoral candidates through the research and writing process. These policies serve as the governing framework that ensures academic rigor, integrity, and compliance with institutional standards. Familiarity with these guidelines allows dissertation chairs to provide structured direction to students, preventing procedural missteps that could delay progress or jeopardize research credibility.

University dissertation policies typically cover various essential aspects, including:

- **Proposal Development and Approval** – Universities often have defined protocols for developing and submitting dissertation proposals, including required elements such as problem statements, literature reviews, and methodological frameworks. Dissertation chairs must ensure that students align their proposals with institutional expectations and receive necessary approvals before advancing to the research phase.

- **Formatting and Submission Requirements** – Institutions maintain specific formatting rules for dissertations, including citation styles, page margins, font usage, and required sections such as abstracts, acknowledgments, and appendices. Chairs should proactively educate students about these standards to prevent last-minute formatting issues.

- **Plagiarism and Academic Integrity** – Many universities employ plagiarism detection software and enforce strict guidelines on citation practices. Dissertation chairs must emphasize the importance of originality, proper attribution of sources, and adherence to ethical research practices.

- **Advisory and Committee Roles** – Institutions often outline specific roles and responsibilities for dissertation chairs and committee members, including meeting frequency, feedback expectations, and voting procedures for dissertation approval. Chairs must be well-versed in these responsibilities to coordinate effectively with committee members [42].

By maintaining a clear understanding of university dissertation policies, dissertation chairs can guide students through each phase of the dissertation process, ensuring adherence to institutional standards while fostering academic excellence.

Compliance with Institutional Review Board (IRB) and Academic Review Board (ARB)

Ensuring compliance with Institutional Review Board (IRB) and Academic Review Board (ARB) regulations is one of the most critical responsibilities of a dissertation chair. These regulatory bodies play a pivotal role in safeguarding ethical research practices, particularly when human subjects are involved.

- **Institutional Review Board (IRB)** – The IRB evaluates research proposals to ensure that studies involving human participants adhere to ethical standards, including informed consent, risk minimization, and data confidentiality [43]. Dissertation chairs must guide students through the IRB submission process, helping them draft comprehensive protocols, secure necessary approvals, and address ethical considerations specific to their research.

- **Academic Review Board (ARB)** – The ARB often oversees the broader academic rigor of dissertation projects, ensuring that research proposals meet institutional expectations regarding theoretical contributions, methodological soundness, and disciplinary relevance. Chairs should work closely with students to refine research questions, justify methodologies, and align studies with institutional academic standards.

To facilitate smooth IRB and ARB approval, dissertation chairs should:

- Encourage students to begin the IRB approval process early, as reviews can be time-consuming.

- Assist in the preparation of required documentation, including informed consent forms, risk assessments, and ethical justification statements.

- Provide students with examples of successfully approved IRB and ARB applications for reference.

- Help students navigate potential ethical dilemmas and revise their protocols as needed.

By ensuring strict compliance with IRB and ARB regulations, dissertation chairs protect the integrity of student research and uphold the university's commitment to ethical scholarship.

Dissertation Timelines and Milestone Tracking

Dissertation chairs play an instrumental role in establishing and maintaining structured dissertation timelines to ensure timely progress and completion. Given the complexity and length of the dissertation process, implementing clear milestone tracking systems is essential.

- **Developing a Dissertation Timeline** – A well-structured dissertation timeline serves as a roadmap that guides students through key phases, including topic selection, literature review, research design, data collection, analysis, writing, and final defense. Chairs should collaborate with students to develop realistic timelines that align with university deadlines while accommodating individual research challenges.

- **Setting Key Milestones** – Breaking down the dissertation process into manageable milestones helps students maintain steady progress. Common milestones include:

  1. Proposal Submission and Approval

  2. IRB Approval (if applicable)

  3. Data Collection and Preliminary Analysis

  4. Drafting and Revising Dissertation Chapters

  5. Dissertation Defense Preparation

  6. Final Submission and Formatting Compliance

- **Monitoring Progress and Addressing Delays** – Dissertation chairs must monitor student progress through regular check-ins, status updates, and structured progress reports. If students encounter obstacles, chairs should provide targeted guidance, recommend time management strategies, and, when necessary, adjust timelines to ensure steady advancement.

- **Leveraging Technology for Tracking** – Many institutions provide digital tools, such as dissertation management platforms, progress-tracking software, and shared document repositories, to help students stay organized [44]. Chairs should familiarize students with these resources to facilitate efficient tracking and communication.

A proactive approach to timeline management and milestone tracking ensures that doctoral candidates remain focused, accountable, and consistently moving toward dissertation completion.

Conclusion

Navigating academic and institutional guidelines is a fundamental aspect of dissertation leadership. A dissertation chair who is well-versed in university policies, IRB and ARB compliance, and structured timeline management serves as an essential pillar of support for doctoral candidates. By fostering a clear understanding of these regulatory and procedural frameworks, dissertation chairs empower students to conduct rigorous, ethical, and timely research, ultimately contributing to scholarly excellence and institutional integrity.

From Philosophy to Policy: Operationalizing Ethical Leadership

Doctoral mentorship does not occur in abstraction. It operates within institutional systems—policies, review boards, formatting standards, compliance procedures, committee structures, and accreditation frameworks. While Chapter 1 challenged your internal orientation toward power and Chapter 2 examined your moment-to-moment decision making, Chapter 3 turns your attention outward.

Good intentions are not enough.

You may be a reflective, ethical, student-centered chair. But if you are unfamiliar with institutional procedures, unclear about committee governance, inconsistent in documentation, or misaligned with compliance expectations, you create risk—for your student, for yourself, and for the institution.

Confusion at the policy level becomes delay at the student level.
Ambiguity at the governance level becomes tension at the committee level.
Ignorance of procedure becomes preventable attrition.

The most effective dissertation chairs understand that structure is not bureaucracy—it is protection. Institutional guidelines exist to preserve rigor, ensure fairness, safeguard research participants, and create procedural equity. When chairs master these systems, students move forward with clarity rather than uncertainty.

Professional doctoral leadership requires three competencies:

1. Institutional fluency

2. Role clarity

3. Ethical compliance

Without these, even well-meaning mentorship becomes inconsistent.

The following onboarding checklist is designed as a systems audit. It is not optional reading—it is operational grounding. Before you assume responsibility for a doctoral candidate, you must ensure you are fully aligned with the institutional architecture within which that candidate must succeed.

If you cannot articulate the rules, timelines, committee authority structures, documentation expectations, and compliance standards, you are not yet prepared to lead.

Excellence in doctoral mentorship is not only relational. It is procedural.

Dissertation Chair Onboarding Checklist

A. Institutional Alignment

☐ Review current university dissertation handbook.

☐ Confirm formatting and submission requirements.

☐ Review IRB and ARB policies.

☐ Confirm committee composition rules.

☐ Understand grievance and appeal procedures.

☐ Review program-specific timeline expectations.

B. Role Clarification

☐ Define chair vs. committee member responsibilities.

☐ Establish response time standards.

☐ Clarify voting procedures for proposal/defense.

☐ Understand documentation requirements.

☐ Confirm student evaluation criteria.

C. Ethical & Professional Standards

☐ Review conflict-of-interest policies.

☐ Review authorship and publication expectations.

☐ Establish AI usage policy alignment.

☐ Review confidentiality expectations.

D. Resource Familiarization

☐ Locate university writing center/dissertation support services

☐ Review available research databases and tools

☐ Identify statistical/methodology consulting resources

☐ Confirm library liaison for student support

☐ Review mental health and student wellness resources

Chapter 4 - Ethical Considerations in Dissertation Supervision

Figure 4. [222].

In the intricate landscape of doctoral research, where intellectual rigor converges with the pursuit of knowledge, ethical considerations serve as the foundation upon which academic integrity is built. At its core, dissertation supervision is not merely about guiding students through methodological complexities, theoretical frameworks, or the mechanics of academic writing; it is about fostering a culture of ethical scholarship, ensuring that research is conducted with transparency, accountability, and an unwavering commitment to the principles of integrity.

The dissertation chair, as the cornerstone of doctoral mentorship, plays a pivotal role in instilling ethical discipline, both in research design and in scholarly conduct. The responsibility of ensuring that research adheres to ethical guidelines extends beyond compliance with institutional policies; it demands a proactive and vigilant approach to mentoring students in the nuanced responsibilities of academic honesty, responsible authorship, and the conscientious treatment of research participants.

As the dissertation progresses from its initial conception to its final defense, ethical dilemmas may emerge—some overt and easily addressed, others subtle and requiring careful judgment. The ethical landscape of doctoral research is fraught with challenges: issues of plagiarism, authorship disputes, data manipulation, conflicts of interest, and the ethical treatment of human subjects. How these concerns are managed speaks to the broader academic culture of integrity and the role of faculty in shaping responsible scholars.

This chapter provides dissertation chairs with a comprehensive guide to navigating these ethical considerations, outlining best practices for maintaining research integrity, preventing misconduct, and fostering a climate of ethical awareness that extends beyond the dissertation process.

Maintaining Academic Integrity and Avoiding Conflicts of Interest

Academic integrity is the cornerstone of scholarly research, and dissertation chairs bear a profound responsibility in upholding these standards. A chair must ensure that both the student's research and their own guidance adhere to the highest ethical principles, fostering a culture of honesty, transparency, and intellectual rigor.

One of the most significant ethical challenges in dissertation supervision is avoiding conflicts of interest. Chairs must be vigilant in maintaining objectivity, ensuring that their personal or professional interests do not interfere with the student's research trajectory. For instance, faculty members should refrain from pressuring students to conform to a particular theoretical perspective simply because it aligns with their own research agenda. Instead, they must create an environment where students can explore diverse methodologies and develop independent scholarly voices.

Additionally, chairs must be cautious in relationships that may pose ethical dilemmas, such as situations where a dissertation chair has a prior personal or business relationship with the student. Universities often have policies that prohibit supervising research where conflicts of interest may arise [45]. To mitigate these risks, transparency is key. If a potential conflict is identified, the chair should disclose it to the appropriate institutional review board and take necessary steps to ensure fairness in the dissertation evaluation process.

Dissertation chairs must also model and enforce academic integrity by promoting proper citation practices, discouraging plagiarism, and ensuring that research findings are accurately reported [46]. They should educate students on ethical writing and research practices, guiding them on how to engage with source material responsibly and avoid unintentional academic misconduct.

Ethical Research Practices and Student Advocacy

Ethical research practices extend beyond proper citation and attribution; they encompass every stage of the research process, from data collection to the dissemination of findings. Dissertation chairs play a pivotal role in guiding students through these ethical considerations, ensuring that their research meets institutional and disciplinary standards.

One critical aspect of ethical research is adherence to Institutional Review Board (IRB) guidelines, particularly when human subjects are involved [47]. Chairs must ensure that students understand and comply with protocols related to informed consent, participant confidentiality, and risk mitigation. Ethical oversight also includes reinforcing the importance of unbiased data collection and reporting, emphasizing that research integrity must take precedence over the pursuit of specific outcomes.

Beyond compliance, dissertation chairs serve as advocates for their students. This means not only ensuring that research meets ethical standards but also fostering an academic culture where students feel supported in navigating challenges. Advocacy can take many forms, including:

- Encouraging students to seek institutional resources for ethical dilemmas.

- Protecting students from undue pressure to alter research findings to fit a desired narrative.

- Providing mentorship that prioritizes the student's intellectual growth over external research agendas.

- Ensuring students receive fair and impartial treatment from committee members and institutional bodies.

By acting as both mentors and advocates, dissertation chairs help students develop a deep appreciation for ethical scholarship while empowering them to conduct meaningful and responsible research.

Confidentiality in Dissertation Review and Faculty-Student Relationships

Maintaining confidentiality is an essential ethical obligation in dissertation supervision. As students entrust dissertation chairs with drafts, data, and research insights, it is the chair's duty to ensure that sensitive information remains protected. Breaching confidentiality can compromise academic integrity, jeopardize the student's work, and even lead to legal ramifications.

Confidentiality in dissertation review pertains to multiple aspects, including:

- **Protecting Research Data:** If a dissertation involves proprietary or unpublished research, chairs must ensure that this information is not disclosed to external parties without the student's consent.

- **Committee Deliberations:** Discussions regarding the student's progress, feedback, and evaluation must remain within the confines of the dissertation committee to maintain fairness and objectivity.

- **Feedback Sensitivity:** Dissertation chairs must exercise discretion when providing feedback, ensuring that constructive criticism is delivered professionally and privately.

In addition to research confidentiality, maintaining appropriate faculty-student relationships is crucial. While mentorship often involves close collaboration, chairs must uphold professional boundaries that prevent favoritism or inappropriate interactions. Ethical supervision necessitates impartiality, ensuring that all students receive equal access to mentorship and opportunities regardless of personal rapport.

Faculty-student relationships must also align with institutional policies, which may include restrictions on dual roles (e.g., a chair serving as both an employer and academic advisor to the same student) [48]. Chairs should familiarize themselves with these guidelines and seek institutional guidance when navigating complex mentorship scenarios.

Trauma-Informed Mentorship: Balancing Confidentiality with Compassion

In the realm of dissertation supervision, the principle of confidentiality is rightly held as sacrosanct. Protecting a student's research ideas, personal disclosures, and professional reputation is foundational to ethical mentoring. But confidentiality—while necessary—is not sufficient. As faculty chairs, we must also cultivate emotional discernment, particularly when working with students who carry academic trauma, chronic stress, or anxiety disorders—conditions increasingly common in the modern doctoral landscape.

Understanding Trauma in the Doctoral Context

Trauma in academia is not always the result of dramatic or isolated events. More often, it is cumulative and systemic—a byproduct of repeated experiences of dismissal, invisibility, over-surveillance, or intellectual invalidation [49]. Students may arrive in our programs already burdened by:

- Racial or gender-based microaggressions in past educational settings
- Previous encounters with unsupportive or abusive advisors
- Cultural alienation or impostor syndrome amplified by elitist academic norms
- PTSD or anxiety that has been dismissed or penalized under the guise of "rigor"

These experiences often go unnamed. But they do not go unfelt. And when we ignore them in the name of "maintaining professional distance," we risk perpetuating the very harm our students are working so hard to overcome.

The Ethical Imperative: Distance with Awareness

Traditional mentoring models emphasize the importance of boundaries, and rightly so. Chairs must avoid inappropriate emotional entanglement, dual relationships, or attempts to be a student's therapist. But trauma-informed mentorship challenges us to rethink what professional distance actually means.

It does *not* mean emotional detachment.
It does *not* mean ignoring signs of distress.
It does *not* mean reciting policy instead of extending humanity.

It means holding space with care and containment. It means knowing when to refer, when to listen, and when to intervene with structure and empathy. Most importantly, it means seeing the student as a whole human being, not just a vessel for intellectual output.

Practicing Trauma-Informed Confidentiality

Being trauma-informed in supervision does not require deep clinical training. It requires presence, humility, and consistency. Here are core practices to integrate into your mentoring approach:

- **Anticipate silence as a signal**: A disengaged student may not be "lazy"—they may be in cognitive overload or emotional shutdown due to unresolved academic trauma.
- **Respond to vulnerability without re-traumatization**: If a student shares that they are overwhelmed, avoid phrases like "That's just part of the process." Instead, validate the emotion while offering structure: "It's understandable you're feeling that way. Let's map out the next steps together."
- **Use clarity as a tool for safety**: Predictable timelines, clear expectations, and written feedback reduce ambiguity—which is often a trigger for anxious or trauma-impacted students.
- **Maintain student dignity during delays or setbacks**: Don't mock, shame, or compare. Every scholar's nervous system and life circumstance are different.

Case in Point: Ethical Awareness in Action

A doctoral student misses two scheduled check-ins, then sends an email saying they're "struggling but don't want to bother anyone."

A trauma-uninformed response: "We all struggle. You need to manage your time better."

A trauma-informed response: "Thanks for reaching out. I want to make sure you feel supported. Let's meet briefly to check in—not just on the dissertation, but on how you're managing overall. If there are other supports you need, I can help you get connected."

This is not therapy. It's ethical mentorship rooted in humanity.

The Takeaway

Confidentiality is not just about protecting information—it's about protecting trust. Trauma-informed chairs understand that power, privilege, and academic tradition can all contribute to silent harm. And they commit to supervision practices that are grounded in clarity, softened by compassion, and attuned to the lived experiences of those they mentor.

When you choose to see beyond the dissertation—to see the person—you are not crossing a boundary. You are honoring the sacred work of mentorship.

Conclusion

Ethical dissertation supervision is not a static checklist—it is a dynamic, relational commitment. As we've explored in this chapter, the heart of doctoral mentorship lies not just in upholding rules or policies, but in embodying mature, conscious leadership that safeguards both scholarly integrity and human dignity.

Whether navigating conflicts of interest, balancing confidentiality with transparency, or ensuring equity across committee processes, your ethical stance as a chair becomes a modeling mechanism. Students don't just learn research skills from you—they learn what ethical power looks like in practice.

But perhaps the deepest ethical call-in dissertation mentorship is one of presence. To be present with a struggling student. To maintain boundaries while also showing compassion. To remain vigilant for unconscious bias, academic elitism, or subtle coercion masquerading as tradition. To admit when you are unsure, and to seek alignment before exerting authority.

Ethics in this context is not abstract—it is profoundly personal.

It's the tone of your email when a student is late.
It's the silence you choose when a committee member speaks with unnecessary harshness.
It's the invitation you extend when a student doubts their worth.

In the end, doctoral mentorship is not just about producing rigorous research—it's about forming *ethical researchers*. And that formation begins with you.

So ask yourself, not once, but often:

- Am I mentoring in a way that I would want to be mentored?
- Am I honoring both the dissertation and the person writing it?
- Am I creating a climate of courage, fairness, and trust?

When the answer is yes, you are not merely supervising.
You are shaping the future of the academy—one student, one decision, one ethical moment at a time.

From Reflection to Responsibility: Defining the Standard of Chair Leadership

The first section of this book has asked you to examine yourself before examining a student.

You have been challenged to confront inherited norms, interrogate your assumptions about rigor, reconsider how power functions in doctoral education, and reflect on whether your mentorship builds scholars—or simply tests endurance. Reflection, however, is only the beginning.

Awareness without structure produces good intentions.
Structure without awareness produces bureaucracy.

Transformational doctoral leadership requires both.

Before moving into the procedural mechanics of proposal development, research design, IRB navigation, committee coordination, and defense preparation, it is necessary to define the standard you are expected to meet. Not a vague expectation of being "supportive." Not a generic call to "maintain rigor." But a clear articulation of the competencies that distinguish a reactive chair from a deliberate one.

The role of dissertation chair is not administrative. It is developmental. It is not clerical. It is formative. You are responsible for intellectual alignment, ethical judgment, scholarly reasoning, institutional fluency, and structured accountability. These capacities are not assumed simply because you hold a terminal degree.

They must be named.

The following competency model defines the professional standard for doctoral chair leadership. It synthesizes the themes of Section 1 into seven observable capabilities. As you review them, assess honestly where you are strong—and where development is required.

This is not a symbolic framework. It is a performance expectation.

The chapters that follow will build these competencies in practice.

Refined Chair Competency Model
The Transformational Dissertation Chair Framework

To elevate the manuscript from strong guidance to a formal faculty development architecture, the competencies should be clearly defined, behaviorally anchored, and developmentally sequenced. Below is a refined model with operational clarity.

Core Competencies of a Transformational Dissertation Chair

1. Ethical Calibration

Definition: The ability to align mentorship decisions with principled standards rather than ego, tradition, or emotional reactivity.

Demonstrated Through:

- Transparent expectations and consistent standards
- Fair, documented decision-making
- Trauma-informed mentorship practices
- Appropriate boundary setting
- Proactive ethical risk identification (IRB, authorship, power dynamics)

Why It Matters:
Without ethical calibration, rigor becomes rigidity and mentorship becomes control.

2. Structural Alignment

Definition: The capacity to ensure coherence across problem, purpose, theory, methodology, timeline, and institutional requirements.

Demonstrated Through:

- Early detection of design misalignment
- Enforcing proposal readiness gates
- Clear milestone tracking
- Feasibility assessment
- Integration of ARB and IRB readiness processes

Why It Matters:
Most dissertation failures stem from structural drift, not student incapacity.

3. Argumentation Coaching

Definition: The ability to develop doctoral-level reasoning, not just improve writing mechanics.

Demonstrated Through:

- Teaching claim–warrant–evidence logic
- Challenging unsupported assertions
- Requiring theoretical grounding
- Conducting mini-defenses
- Strengthening counterargument integration

Why It Matters:
A dissertation is not a document. It is an argument.

4. Feedback Precision

Definition: Delivering actionable, prioritized, and development-oriented feedback that accelerates progress.

Demonstrated Through:

- Specific, referenced critique
- Clear revision guidance
- Balanced tone
- Differentiation between major and minor issues
- Defined turnaround expectations

Why It Matters:
Vague feedback extends timelines and erodes confidence.

5. Institutional Fluency

Definition: Mastery of policies, governance structures, and compliance systems that shape the dissertation process.

Demonstrated Through:

- Understanding committee rules and voting procedures
- Accurate IRB/ARB submission guidance
- Clear escalation pathways
- Proper documentation practices
- Adherence to formatting and submission standards

Why It Matters:
Confusion at the policy level becomes delay at the student level.

6. AI-Era Judgment

Definition: The discernment to guide responsible AI integration while preserving intellectual ownership.

Demonstrated Through:

- Clear AI usage expectations
- Distinguishing support from substitution
- Evaluating authorship integrity
- Teaching ethical tool use

- Modeling AI-assisted scholarship responsibly

Why It Matters:
The doctoral landscape has changed. Supervision must evolve without surrendering standards.

7. Performance Intervention Leadership

Definition: The ability to address stagnation, professionalism concerns, or academic deficiencies with structure and fairness.

Demonstrated Through:

- Evidence-based performance conversations
- Clear behavioral expectations
- Support resource identification
- Action plans with benchmarks
- Understanding formal escalation processes

Why It Matters:
Avoidance compounds dysfunction. Structured accountability restores progress.

Section 2: The Dissertation Process from Start to Finish

The first step in reshaping doctoral mentorship begins not with your students—but with yourself. Section 1 asked you to confront your own academic lineage, your unspoken assumptions, and the habits—both empowering and harmful—that you carry into your role as chair. It invited you to see mentorship not as a static task, but as a dynamic legacy shaped by every meeting, every comment, every silence.

But insight without application is inertia.

Now that you've begun the work of self-reflection, the next step is to turn that inward clarity into outward connection. Because doctoral success is not built on checklists—it is built on relationships.

The faculty-student relationship in doctoral education is unlike any other. It is long-term, high-stakes, emotionally complex, and often deeply personal. It requires both structure and care, boundaries and belief. And too often, it suffers from miscommunication, mismatched expectations, or subtle power imbalances that go unaddressed until they fracture trust—or derail progress [50].

Figure S2. [222].

In the chapters that follow, we'll shift from internal reflection to interpersonal strategy. You'll learn how to establish clarity from the beginning, set a tone of professional warmth, and foster trust without dependency. You'll explore how to support diverse learners, navigate difficult conversations, and build a mentorship model that is both ethical and empowering.

Because if Section 1 was about unlocking the master key within you, Section 2 is about learning how to use that key to open the door for someone else.

Chapter 5 - Guiding Students Through Topic Selection & Research Design

Figure 5. [222].

The genesis of any meaningful dissertation lies in its foundation—a well-conceived research topic that is not only intellectually stimulating but also methodologically feasible, theoretically grounded, and relevant to the broader academic discourse. As dissertation chairs, faculty members assume a pivotal role in guiding students through the intricate process of identifying a viable research topic and structuring a rigorous research design. This process is far more than an academic exercise; it is the cornerstone of doctoral scholarship, influencing the quality, depth, and impact of the research that follows.

For doctoral students, the initial phase of dissertation development is often fraught with uncertainty. Faced with an expansive universe of potential research questions, students must navigate a delicate balance between personal intellectual curiosity and the pragmatic considerations of scope, methodology, and scholarly contribution. It is here that the dissertation chair becomes not merely an advisor but a compass—helping students refine vague ideas into concrete research problems, ensuring alignment between inquiry and methodology, and fostering an appreciation for the iterative nature of scholarly investigation.

In this chapter, we explore the essential components of topic selection and research design, detailing strategies for guiding students through each step with intellectual rigor and methodological precision. We examine the importance of ensuring alignment between the research problem, purpose, and methodology, discuss ways to cultivate originality while maintaining feasibility, and address common pitfalls that students encounter in the early stages of their research.

Ultimately, the role of the dissertation chair in this phase is not to dictate topics or impose rigid research frameworks but to serve as a facilitator—prompting students to think critically, challenge assumptions, and refine their ideas into structured, researchable inquiries. In doing so, chairs empower students to produce research that is not only academically sound but also impactful, innovative, and relevant to the evolving landscape of knowledge.

Identifying Viable Research Problems

The foundation of a successful dissertation lies in the selection of a research problem that is both meaningful and viable. Dissertation chairs play an instrumental role in guiding students through this critical phase, ensuring that their chosen topic is well-grounded in existing scholarship while contributing new knowledge to the field.

A viable research problem should meet several essential criteria:

1. **Relevance to the Field:** The problem should address a gap in the literature, align with current debates, and have scholarly or practical significance.

2. **Feasibility within Program Constraints:** Students must be able to complete the research within the timeframe and resources available to them.

3. **Theoretical and Methodological Foundation:** The problem should lend itself to established theoretical frameworks and research methodologies, ensuring a structured approach to inquiry.

4. **Clarity and Focus:** A well-defined research problem avoids excessive breadth while maintaining depth, allowing the student to develop a coherent argument [51].

To support students in identifying a researchable problem, dissertation chairs should encourage an iterative approach, prompting students to explore broad interests before refining their focus. This can be facilitated through:

- **Literature Reviews:** Encouraging students to conduct preliminary literature reviews to identify gaps and areas of contention.

- **Concept Mapping:** Using visual tools to explore connections between different research interests and potential problem statements.

- **Research Question Development:** Guiding students to draft and refine research questions that are clear, specific, and researchable.

- **Scholarly Discussions:** Engaging in structured conversations that challenge students to justify the significance of their proposed research.

By fostering a structured yet flexible exploration of research problems, dissertation chairs empower students to select topics that are both original and feasible.

Ensuring Alignment Between Problem, Purpose, and Methodology

Once a research problem has been identified, ensuring a strong alignment between the problem, purpose, and methodology is paramount to the success of the dissertation. Misalignment between these elements can lead to methodological inconsistencies, unclear findings, and a weaker overall study.

- **The Research Problem:** This defines the issue being investigated and provides the rationale for why the study is necessary.

- **The Purpose Statement:** This articulates the intent of the study and the expected contribution to knowledge or practice.

- **The Methodology:** This determines how the study will be conducted, including data collection and analysis strategies.

To achieve alignment, dissertation chairs should guide students through structured questioning, such as:

- Does the research problem logically lead to the stated purpose of the study?

- Does the methodology adequately address the research problem and purpose?

- Are the research questions or hypotheses explicitly tied to the problem and purpose?

- Is the methodology appropriate for the type of data required to answer the research questions?

Alignment can be further reinforced by encouraging students to develop a methodology rationale, wherein they explicitly justify their methodological choices in relation to the problem and purpose [52]. Chairs should also recommend iterative refinements, ensuring coherence between conceptual, theoretical, and methodological elements before formalizing the dissertation proposal.

Encouraging Originality While Maintaining Feasibility

Doctoral research should contribute to the academic field by presenting new perspectives, advancing theoretical frameworks, or applying methodologies in novel ways [53]. However, originality must be balanced with feasibility to ensure that the study remains realistic given the student's time, expertise, and available resources.

Strategies for encouraging originality include:

- **Expanding Theoretical Perspectives:** Encouraging students to build upon existing theories in new ways or integrate interdisciplinary frameworks.

- **Employing Novel Methodologies:** Exploring less commonly used research methods or mixed-methods approaches that yield richer insights.

- **Identifying Underexplored Areas:** Guiding students to investigate populations, variables, or phenomena that have received limited scholarly attention.

- **Practical Application:** Encouraging applied research that addresses real-world problems in innovative ways [54].

At the same time, dissertation chairs must temper ambitious research ideas with practical considerations. This includes ensuring that:

- Data collection is feasible within the given timeframe.

- Ethical and institutional review board (IRB) approvals are attainable.

- The chosen methodology is within the student's technical capacity.

- The scope of the study is appropriate for a doctoral dissertation rather than a multi-year research project [55].

By helping students strike the right balance between innovation and feasibility, dissertation chairs ensure that research remains both impactful and realistically executable.

Conclusion

Guiding students through topic selection and research design is one of the most crucial responsibilities of a dissertation chair. By facilitating the identification of viable research problems, ensuring alignment between problem, purpose, and methodology, and fostering originality while maintaining feasibility, chairs set the stage for successful dissertation research. A well-chosen and well-structured research topic not only enhances the student's academic experience but also contributes meaningfully to the broader field of scholarship.

Structural Integrity Before Advancement

By the time a doctoral student reaches the end of Chapters 1–3, something critical has already been decided—whether the study is structurally sound or structurally unstable.

Most dissertations do not derail during data collection. They do not collapse during analysis. They rarely fail at the defense because of presentation. They struggle because foundational misalignment went uncorrected early.

An unclear problem. A vague theoretical frame. A methodology that does not answer the questions posed. A scope that exceeds feasibility.

When these weaknesses pass through proposal approval, the chair is no longer guiding refinement— the chair is managing damage. Your responsibility at this stage is not encouragement. It is calibration.

Chapters 1–3 represent the architectural blueprint of the study. If the blueprint is flawed, construction cannot proceed. Advancement to proposal defense should never be based on effort, personality, or optimism. It must be based on coherence, alignment, and feasibility.

This checklist is a structural integrity audit.

It allows you to evaluate whether:

- The conceptual foundation is defensible.
- The literature grounding is credible.
- The design is logically aligned.
- The scope is realistic.
- The ethics are addressed.

It also provides explicit red flags—conditions under which advancement should pause. Not as punishment. Not as gatekeeping. But as protection.

Protection of the student's time. Protection of methodological rigor. Protection of committee credibility. Protection of the institution's scholarly standards.

If even one red flag is present, forward movement is premature. Strong chairs do not approve proposals because they are "close." They approve proposals because they are structurally ready.

Use this checklist as your standard.

Proposal Readiness & Research Design Integrity Checklist

For Dissertation Chairs Reviewing Chapters 1–3

I. Conceptual Foundation (Chapter 1 Integrity)

A. Introduction & Framing

☐ Hook clearly establishes relevance of the study
☐ Background provides contextual grounding (not a literature review)
☐ Problem statement identifies a genuine, researchable gap
☐ Problem is specific, bounded, and defensible
☐ Purpose statement is concise and logically derived from the problem
☐ Research questions are numbered, aligned, and answerable
☐ Significance statement demonstrates both theoretical and practical contribution
☐ Key terms are clearly defined and sourced
☐ Chapter organization preview is present

II. Scholarly Grounding (Literature Command)

☐ Student demonstrates command of foundational literature
☐ Recent scholarship is meaningfully integrated
☐ Research gap is explicitly articulated
☐ Theoretical framework is clearly identified
☐ Theoretical framework is justified relative to the problem
☐ Framework aligns with research questions

III. Design Alignment (Methodological Coherence)

☐ Research design directly addresses research questions
☐ Methodology is appropriate to question type
☐ Design justification is explicitly articulated
☐ Scope is feasible within doctoral timeline
☐ Timeline is realistic and defensible

IV. Population & Sampling Integrity

☐ Population is clearly defined
☐ Sampling strategy is appropriate
☐ Inclusion/exclusion criteria are defensible
☐ Sample size rationale is provided
☐ Access feasibility confirmed

V. Data Collection & Instrumentation

☐ Data collection procedures are replicable
☐ Instruments or interview protocols described or included
☐ Measurement approach aligns with research questions
☐ Data management plan described

VI. Data Analysis Alignment

☐ Analysis plan matches data type
☐ Statistical procedures justified (if quantitative)
☐ Coding/thematic process articulated (if qualitative)
☐ Mixed-method integration explained (if applicable)
☐ Validity/reliability or trustworthiness addressed
☐ Limitations acknowledged

VII. Ethical & Compliance Readiness

☐ Ethical risks identified
☐ Informed consent process described
☐ IRB status clarified
☐ Confidentiality procedures defined

Red Flags — Stop and Revise Before Committee Review

☐ Problem statement is broad, vague, or descriptive
☐ No explicit theoretical framework
☐ Methodology does not align with research questions
☐ Scope exceeds doctoral feasibility
☐ Insufficient recent literature engagement
☐ Analysis plan underdeveloped or misaligned
☐ No clear contribution articulated

If any red flag is present, proposal advancement should pause.

Chapter 6 - Supporting Literature Review Development

The literature review is a foundational component of the dissertation, serving as both the intellectual framework and justification for the research study [56]. It establishes the academic context of the research by synthesizing existing studies, identifying gaps in knowledge, and demonstrating the relevance of the dissertation topic. A well-developed literature review strengthens the credibility of the research and provides a roadmap for the study's theoretical and methodological approach.

Doctoral candidates often find the literature review process challenging due to the sheer volume of academic sources, the need for critical analysis, and the requirement to present a coherent narrative. Unlike a simple summary of existing research, a literature review must engage deeply with scholarly debates, compare and contrast perspectives, and highlight unresolved questions that justify the dissertation's contribution. Dissertation chairs play a crucial role in guiding students through this complex process, helping them navigate academic databases, refine their research focus, and develop a structured, analytical literature review [57].

Figure 6. [222].

The key aspects of literature review development include:

- **Teaching Students to Synthesize Scholarly Work** – A literature review must go beyond summarization to integrate and analyze research findings, providing a critical discussion that positions the dissertation within the broader academic conversation.

- **Identifying Research Gaps and Framing Theoretical Foundations** – Effective literature reviews highlight gaps in existing research and justify the need for further investigation, providing a strong rationale for the dissertation's research questions and objectives.

- **Evaluating the Credibility of Sources and Literature Integration** – Selecting high-quality, peer-reviewed sources and maintaining a balanced perspective ensures that the literature review is rigorous, relevant, and methodologically sound [58].

A well-executed literature review enhances the dissertation by ensuring that the research is grounded in established theories and empirical findings. It also prepares students for scholarly publishing by developing their ability to engage with academic literature critically and systematically. Dissertation chairs must mentor students in developing a structured approach to literature synthesis, ensuring that their reviews are comprehensive, methodologically rigorous, and logically organized.

This chapter provides a detailed guide to supporting literature review development in dissertation work. It covers best practices for sourcing academic literature, strategies for synthesizing research effectively, and techniques for identifying gaps that justify the dissertation's research questions. By mastering the principles of literature review development, doctoral candidates can build a strong theoretical and conceptual foundation for their research, enhancing the impact and scholarly value of their dissertation.

Teaching Students to Synthesize Scholarly Work

A well-crafted literature review is far more than a summary of existing research; it is a critical synthesis that contextualizes a student's dissertation within the broader academic discourse [59]. Dissertation chairs must guide students in transforming collections of studies into a cohesive narrative that highlights trends, debates, and scholarly evolution within their field of study.

To facilitate effective synthesis, dissertation chairs should encourage students to:

1. **Identify Key Themes:** Instead of listing articles one by one, students should categorize literature into themes or conceptual frameworks, recognizing patterns across multiple sources.

2. **Compare and Contrast Studies:** Students must analyze similarities and differences in research findings, theoretical approaches, and methodologies to determine areas of consensus and divergence.

3. **Integrate Literature into a Coherent Argument:** A literature review should logically lead to the student's research problem by demonstrating how prior studies contribute to, or fail to address, the identified gap.

4. **Use Synthesis Matrices:** Encouraging the use of synthesis matrices helps students organize and visualize relationships between sources, making it easier to construct a well-integrated review.

5. **Develop a Strong Narrative Flow:** Dissertation chairs should help students structure their reviews logically, using transition statements to create fluidity between themes and studies.

By mastering these synthesis techniques, students can construct literature reviews that provide not just context but also critical analysis, positioning their research within an ongoing scholarly conversation.

Identifying Research Gaps and Framing Theoretical Foundations

One of the central purposes of a literature review is to justify the need for a student's study by identifying research gaps. Dissertation chairs must train students to discern what has been studied, what remains unknown, and where their own research contributes to the advancement of knowledge.

Key strategies for identifying research gaps include:

- **Analyzing Contradictory Findings:** Highlighting inconsistencies in prior research and justifying the need for further exploration.

- **Recognizing Understudied Populations or Contexts:** Encouraging students to identify demographics, industries, or case studies that have been overlooked in existing literature.

- **Addressing Methodological Limitations:** Helping students critique past methodologies and propose more robust or alternative research designs.

- **Spotting Theoretical Weaknesses:** Encouraging students to examine whether dominant theories fully explain phenomena or if new theoretical perspectives are needed.

In framing theoretical foundations, dissertation chairs should guide students in selecting and justifying the theories that will shape their studies. This involves:

- **Choosing Theories that Align with Research Questions:** Ensuring that theoretical frameworks are appropriate for the study's focus.

- **Exploring Interdisciplinary Perspectives:** Encouraging students to integrate theories from multiple disciplines when applicable.

- **Building on Existing Theories:** Advising students on how to extend, refine, or challenge established theoretical models.

By effectively identifying research gaps and establishing a strong theoretical foundation, students can position their work as a meaningful contribution to their academic field.

Evaluating the Credibility of Sources and Literature Integration

The integrity of a dissertation's literature review depends on the credibility of the sources it incorporates. Dissertation chairs must train students to critically assess the quality of their references, ensuring that they rely on reputable, peer-reviewed research rather than unreliable or outdated materials.

Key criteria for evaluating source credibility include:

- **Peer-Reviewed vs. Non-Peer-Reviewed Sources:** Teaching students to distinguish between scholarly articles, grey literature, and non-academic sources.

- **Author Expertise and Institutional Affiliation:** Encouraging scrutiny of an author's credentials and research background.

- **Journal Impact Factor and Reputation:** Directing students toward high-impact journals and well-regarded academic publishers.

- **Publication Date and Relevance:** Ensuring that students prioritize recent research while acknowledging foundational studies.

- **Citations and Influence:** Teaching students to assess an article's credibility based on how frequently it is cited within their field.

Beyond evaluating individual sources, dissertation chairs must emphasize the importance of literature integration, ensuring that students do not merely compile sources but actively weave them into a coherent scholarly argument. Strategies for effective integration include:

- **Avoiding a "Book Report" Approach:** Steering students away from isolated summaries and toward comparative discussions that establish relationships between studies.

- **Using Source Blending:** Encouraging students to incorporate multiple sources into a single discussion point rather than analyzing each source separately.

- **Citing Sources Strategically:** Teaching students when and how to cite sources to strengthen their arguments and avoid unnecessary over-citation.

- **Ensuring Proper Citation Formatting:** Guiding students on APA, MLA, or other relevant citation styles to maintain academic integrity.

By mastering source evaluation and literature integration, students can produce literature reviews that are not only rigorous and well-supported but also deeply insightful and analytically rich.

Conclusion

Supporting students in developing their literature reviews is a fundamental responsibility of dissertation chairs. By teaching students to synthesize scholarly work, identify research gaps, and critically evaluate sources, chairs empower them to construct literature reviews that lay a solid foundation for their dissertation research. A well-developed literature review not only demonstrates mastery of existing scholarship but also sets the stage for the student's original contributions, ensuring that their dissertation holds both academic significance and scholarly integrity.

Chapter 7 - Reviewing Research Methodology

Figure 7. [222].

A dissertation's success is largely determined by the strength of its research methodology [60]. The methodology serves as the foundation of scholarly inquiry, providing the framework for data collection, analysis, and interpretation. A well-defined research methodology ensures that findings are credible, reproducible, and aligned with the research questions. Dissertation chairs play a vital role in guiding students through the selection, justification, and execution of appropriate methodologies, ensuring academic rigor and methodological soundness [61].

Selecting the right methodology is one of the most critical decisions in dissertation research. Whether a study adopts a qualitative, quantitative, or mixed-methods approach, the chosen methodology must align with the research problem, purpose, and objectives. Beyond selecting a methodology, students must demonstrate a clear understanding of research design, sampling techniques, data collection methods, and analytical procedures. Without methodological clarity, research findings may lack validity and reliability, undermining the overall impact of the dissertation [62].

The key aspects of research methodology in dissertation writing include:

- **Assessing Quantitative, Qualitative, and Mixed-Methods Approaches** – Understanding the differences between research methodologies and selecting the most appropriate approach ensures that the study effectively answers the research questions.

- **Sampling, Data Collection, and Analysis Considerations** – Proper selection of study participants, reliable data collection methods, and appropriate analytical techniques contribute to the validity and credibility of the research findings [63].

- **Ensuring Research Methods Align with Study Objectives** – A well-structured methodology must directly support the research purpose and be justified in relation to existing literature and disciplinary norms.

A strong research methodology not only strengthens the dissertation but also prepares students for future scholarly contributions. Dissertation chairs must help students anticipate potential methodological challenges, refine their research design, and justify their choices to ensure alignment with academic expectations. Additionally, adherence to ethical research standards, including Institutional Review Board (IRB) requirements, is crucial in maintaining the integrity of the research process [64].

This chapter provides a comprehensive guide to reviewing and refining research methodologies in dissertation work. It explores the key elements of methodology selection, strategies for ensuring methodological rigor, and best practices for aligning research methods with study objectives. By mastering these principles, doctoral candidates can develop a well-structured methodology that enhances the credibility and scholarly contribution of their research.

Assessing Quantitative, Qualitative, and Mixed-Methods Approaches

Selecting an appropriate research methodology is a cornerstone of the dissertation process, shaping the validity, reliability, and impact of a doctoral candidate's study [65]. Dissertation chairs must guide students in evaluating the strengths, limitations, and applicability of quantitative, qualitative, and mixed-methods approaches, ensuring alignment with their research objectives and questions.

- **Quantitative Research** focuses on numerical data, statistical analysis, and objective measurements. This approach is best suited for studies requiring hypothesis testing, large-scale data collection, and generalizability [66]. Dissertation chairs should help students determine whether their research problem can be addressed through structured instruments such as surveys, experiments, or secondary data analysis. Key considerations include:
  - Selecting appropriate statistical tests based on research questions and data types.
  - Ensuring sample size sufficiency for statistical power.
  - Addressing potential biases in data collection and measurement.

- **Qualitative Research** emphasizes depth over breadth, exploring human experiences, perceptions, and meanings through interviews, case studies, ethnographies, or textual analyses. This approach is ideal for research that seeks to understand complex phenomena, social interactions, or cultural contexts. Dissertation chairs should guide students in:
  - Developing rigorous coding and thematic analysis strategies.
  - Ensuring reflexivity and transparency in data interpretation.
  - Justifying methodological choices based on epistemological foundations.

- **Mixed-Methods Research** integrates both quantitative and qualitative approaches to provide a comprehensive understanding of a research problem. This approach is particularly useful for studies requiring both statistical measurement and contextual interpretation [67]. Chairs must support students in:
  - Designing a coherent research framework that integrates both methods effectively.
  - Balancing the challenges of dual-method data collection and analysis.
  - Addressing potential conflicts between qualitative insights and quantitative trends.

By thoroughly assessing these methodological approaches, dissertation chairs help students make informed decisions that strengthen the credibility and contribution of their research.

Sampling, Data Collection, and Analysis Considerations

Once the research methodology is determined, dissertation chairs must ensure that students apply rigorous sampling, data collection, and analysis techniques that align with their chosen approach. Effective methodological design enhances the reliability, validity, and ethical integrity of the dissertation.

- **Sampling Strategies**

    - **Probability Sampling (e.g., random, stratified, cluster sampling):** Common in quantitative research, these techniques ensure representativeness and generalizability [68].

    - **Non-Probability Sampling (e.g., purposive, snowball, convenience sampling):** Often used in qualitative research, these methods facilitate in-depth exploration but require careful justification [69].

    - **Sample Size Considerations:** Chairs should guide students in determining appropriate sample sizes based on statistical power for quantitative studies or thematic saturation for qualitative studies [70].

- **Data Collection Techniques**

    - **Surveys and Questionnaires:** Require careful instrument validation and pilot testing [71].

    - **Interviews and Focus Groups:** Must ensure robust protocols for question structuring, participant engagement, and transcription accuracy [72].

    - **Observations and Case Studies:** Require systematic frameworks for recording and analyzing qualitative data [73].

    - **Archival and Secondary Data Analysis:** Must address data reliability, access limitations, and contextual applicability [74].

- **Data Analysis Approaches**

    - **Quantitative Analysis:** Requires appropriate statistical techniques, ranging from descriptive statistics to complex inferential models such as regression analysis, ANOVA, or structural equation modeling [75].

    - **Qualitative Analysis:** Demands structured coding techniques, thematic analysis, and frameworks such as grounded theory or discourse analysis [76].

    - **Mixed-Methods Integration:** Calls for a clear articulation of how qualitative insights complement or contrast with quantitative findings [77].

By emphasizing methodological rigor and alignment, dissertation chairs can ensure that students employ robust techniques that yield meaningful and defensible research outcomes.

Ensuring Research Methods Align with Study Objectives

A fundamental challenge for doctoral students is ensuring that their research methods align seamlessly with their study objectives, research questions, and theoretical framework. Dissertation chairs play a pivotal role in preventing methodological misalignment, which can weaken the study's coherence and validity.

Key strategies for maintaining alignment include:

- **Clarifying Research Questions and Hypotheses:**

    - Chairs should ensure that students articulate clear, focused research questions that logically dictate their methodological approach.

    - Quantitative studies should have testable hypotheses, whereas qualitative studies should have exploratory questions designed to uncover nuanced insights [78].

- **Mapping Methodological Decisions to Study Goals:**

    - Each component of the methodology (sampling, data collection, analysis) should directly contribute to answering the research questions.

    - Chairs should encourage students to draft detailed methodological rationales that justify their choices in relation to their research objectives.

- **Addressing Feasibility and Practicality:**

    - Research methods should be feasible given the student's time constraints, access to participants, and technical expertise.

    - Ethical considerations, such as participant confidentiality and informed consent, must be integrated into methodological planning [79].

By maintaining a steadfast focus on alignment, dissertation chairs help students develop research methodologies that not only meet academic rigor but also yield meaningful and valid contributions to their field.

Conclusion

Reviewing and refining research methodologies is a critical component of the dissertation process. Dissertation chairs must guide students through selecting appropriate methodological approaches, ensuring robust sampling and data collection techniques, and maintaining methodological alignment with study objectives. Through strategic mentorship, chairs enable doctoral candidates to design and execute research that is methodologically sound, ethically responsible, and academically impactful.

Chapter 8 - Ensuring Strong Writing and Argumentation

Clear, coherent, and rigorous writing is the foundation of a well-crafted dissertation. Doctoral research is not just about conducting an investigation; it is about communicating findings effectively, making compelling arguments, and demonstrating academic excellence. Dissertation chairs must guide students in refining their writing to ensure clarity, logical progression, and scholarly rigor throughout their work. Writing at the doctoral level requires precision, a structured approach to argumentation, and the ability to synthesize complex ideas in a way that is both persuasive and academically sound.

Dissertation writing is a unique and demanding process that requires careful attention to detail, from formulating research questions to presenting conclusions [80]. Many doctoral candidates struggle with maintaining coherence, organizing their arguments effectively, and ensuring their writing meets the standards of academic scholarship [81]. Without strong writing and argumentation skills, even the most well-researched dissertation can fail to make a significant contribution to the field [82].

Figure 8. [222].

The key aspects of strong dissertation writing and argumentation include:

- **Reviewing Drafts for Clarity, Coherence, and Rigor** – Ensuring that ideas are expressed clearly, transitions between sections are smooth, and arguments are logically structured enhances the overall readability and impact of the dissertation.

- **Teaching Students How to Construct a Strong Academic Argument** – Developing well-supported claims, grounding arguments in scholarly research, and integrating evidence effectively help strengthen the dissertation's overall persuasiveness.

- **Identifying Common Pitfalls in Dissertation Writing** – Addressing issues such as redundancy, weak argumentation, unclear thesis statements, and disorganized content ensures that the dissertation remains well-structured and compelling.

Strong dissertation writing does not happen in isolation; it requires continuous refinement, feedback, and the application of best practices in academic composition. Dissertation chairs play a crucial role in providing constructive feedback, guiding students through the revision process, and helping them enhance their writing skills.

This chapter explores the essential elements of strong academic writing and argumentation in dissertation work. It provides practical strategies for improving clarity, organizing research logically, and developing persuasive arguments. By mastering these skills, doctoral candidates can present their research with confidence and contribute meaningfully to their academic discipline.

Reviewing Drafts for Clarity, Coherence, and Rigor

A well-crafted dissertation is not merely a collection of research findings but a meticulously structured scholarly document that demonstrates clarity, coherence, and intellectual rigor. Dissertation chairs play a pivotal role in guiding students through iterative drafts, helping them refine their ideas and enhance the overall readability and scholarly impact of their work.

To ensure clarity, dissertation chairs should encourage students to:

- **Write with precision and conciseness:** Avoiding verbose and ambiguous language ensures arguments remain direct and comprehensible.

- **Define key terms early:** Establishing clear definitions prevents misinterpretations and strengthens conceptual clarity.

- **Maintain logical flow:** Each section should transition smoothly into the next, preventing disjointed discussions.

- **Use straightforward sentence structures:** Overly complex phrasing can obscure meaning, making it harder for readers to follow the argument.

Coherence in writing is achieved by maintaining thematic consistency throughout the dissertation [83]. Dissertation chairs should help students:

- **Develop strong topic sentences for each paragraph:** Each paragraph should convey a single, clear idea that contributes to the overall argument.

- **Ensure paragraph transitions are smooth:** Logical connectors and bridging sentences help maintain a seamless flow.

- **Avoid redundancy and contradictions:** Repeating information dilutes the strength of the argument, while contradictions undermine its validity.

Rigor in dissertation writing requires precision, evidence-based argumentation, and thorough engagement with literature [84]. To enhance rigor, students should:

- **Ground arguments in scholarly literature:** Citing authoritative sources strengthens the credibility of claims.

- **Engage critically with different perspectives:** Demonstrating awareness of debates and counterarguments enriches the analysis.

- **Support claims with empirical evidence:** Data-driven arguments lend weight to the study's findings and conclusions.

By fostering clarity, coherence, and rigor, dissertation chairs ensure that students develop manuscripts that meet the highest academic standards.

Teaching Students How to Construct a Strong Academic Argument

A dissertation's impact is largely determined by the strength of its central argument [85]. Students must learn to construct a compelling, well-supported thesis that effectively conveys the significance of their research [86]. Dissertation chairs play a crucial role in cultivating this skill.

Key components of a strong academic argument include:

1. **A clear thesis statement:** The dissertation should present a central argument or hypothesis that is specific, concise, and defensible.

2. **Logical structure and organization:** Arguments should be presented in a systematic, hierarchical manner, progressing logically from foundational premises to advanced interpretations.

3. **Use of evidence and analysis:** Claims must be substantiated with empirical data, theoretical insights, or robust scholarly discussion.

4. **Consideration of counterarguments:** Addressing alternative perspectives strengthens the credibility of the argument and demonstrates academic maturity.

5. **A compelling conclusion:** The dissertation should culminate in a well-reasoned synthesis that reinforces the argument and underscores its contributions to the field.

To instill these principles, dissertation chairs should:

- **Encourage students to draft argument maps:** Visualizing the structure of their argument helps identify gaps and weaknesses.

- **Teach the art of scholarly persuasion:** Students should be guided in using rhetorical strategies such as analogy, contrast, and exemplification to strengthen their case.

- **Refine their ability to articulate significance:** Every claim should be tied to the broader implications of the research, ensuring that arguments are impactful and relevant.

By honing these argumentative techniques, students can craft dissertations that make substantive contributions to their field.

Common Pitfalls in Dissertation Argumentation and How to Address Them

Even the most promising dissertations can be undermined by weaknesses in argumentation [87]. Identifying and addressing these common pitfalls is a crucial aspect of dissertation mentorship.

1. Weak or Unclear Thesis Statements

- **Pitfall:** A vague or overly broad thesis makes it difficult to construct a focused argument.

- **Solution:** Students should refine their thesis to be specific, researchable, and clearly articulated.

2. Unsupported Claims

- **Pitfall:** Assertions made without sufficient evidence weaken credibility.

- **Solution:** Encourage students to substantiate every claim with empirical data, theoretical reasoning, or scholarly references.

3. Logical Fallacies

- **Pitfall:** Errors in reasoning, such as hasty generalizations, straw man arguments, or false dichotomies, can compromise the argument's validity.

- **Solution:** Train students to recognize and avoid logical fallacies through critical review and structured reasoning exercises.

4. Over-Reliance on Description Rather than Analysis

- **Pitfall:** Summarizing existing research without offering original interpretation limits the dissertation's contribution.

- **Solution:** Guide students in developing analytical depth by asking critical questions and encouraging theoretical engagement.

5. Disorganized Presentation of Ideas

- **Pitfall:** A poorly structured dissertation makes it difficult for readers to follow the argument.

- **Solution:** Emphasize the importance of outlining before writing and using clear section headings.

6. Failure to Engage with Counterarguments

- **Pitfall:** Ignoring alternative perspectives weakens argumentative robustness.

- **Solution:** Encourage students to anticipate, acknowledge, and refute counterarguments within their discussion.

By proactively addressing these pitfalls, dissertation chairs equip students with the skills necessary to present well-reasoned, compelling arguments.

AI as Coach, Not Crutch — Navigating the Rise of Generative Tools in Doctoral Writing

The ability to construct a coherent, evidence-based argument is central to doctoral research. But increasingly, students are arriving at the dissertation phase with uneven argumentation skills and now, with access to powerful generative AI tools like ChatGPT, Scite, Grammarly, and Perplexity. These tools can be incredibly useful. They can also be quietly corrosive.

What we're witnessing is not just a shift in writing mechanics, but a deeper epistemological shift: from internal critical reasoning to external cognitive outsourcing.

As faculty chairs, we must learn to mentor within this new reality not by policing AI, but by contextualizing its role. We must teach students how to use these tools with clarity, integrity, and scholarly self-awareness.

The Appeal of AI: Speed, Structure, and the Illusion of Mastery

Doctoral writing is cognitively demanding and emotionally exhausting. Students often face:

- Analysis paralysis
- Perfectionism
- Writer's block
- Fear of being "found out" as not scholarly enough

Generative AI tools offer a tempting remedy. They provide fast, coherent text that sounds academic. They can reframe questions, suggest outlines, and generate citations—some real, some not. This can give students a false sense of fluency, bypassing the developmental struggle necessary to internalize scholarly logic.

But writing is not just output, it is cognition. When a student outsources the cognitive labor of argumentation, they also outsource their growth as a thinker.

The Risks of Over-Reliance

If left unchecked, overuse of AI tools can result in:

- Superficial or formulaic arguments that lack nuance
- Fragmented or logically inconsistent claims
- Erosion of the student's authentic scholarly voice
- Ethical lapses, including hallucinated citations and unattributed paraphrasing [88].

These issues are not always intentional. Most students are not trying to cheat—they're trying to cope. But the result is the same: a diluted dissertation that may meet surface expectations but fails to reflect original, defensible thought.

This is where faculty leadership becomes essential.

A New Mentoring Responsibility: Teaching the Ethical Use of AI

Chairs must begin addressing AI use not as an afterthought, but as an early, intentional part of dissertation planning. Silence creates ambiguity. Ambiguity creates misuse.

During your initial conversations with students—especially in Chapters 1 through 3—include a discussion about their writing process. Ask:

- "Where do you get stuck?"

- "What tools are you using to help yourself think through your ideas?"
- "What do you understand as appropriate use of AI in scholarly work?"

These questions are not accusatory—they are clarifying. They open space for honest discussion and ethical development.

Mentoring practice tip:
Frame AI as a cognitive partner, not a ghostwriter. Emphasize that using AI to clarify ideas is not the same as having it generate entire sections of text or rationale.

Understanding AI as a Cognitive Tool: Coach vs. Crutch

To help both students and faculty distinguish between healthy use and unhealthy dependence, consider this guiding metaphor:

AI as Coach	**AI as Crutch**
Supports critical thinking	Replaces critical thinking
Aids in revision and brainstorming	Drafts full sections without engagement
Offers structure to clarify ideas	Fills gaps the student doesn't understand
Requires verification and synthesis	Outputs unverifiable or false claims
Enhances voice and organization	Erodes voice and originality

Conclusion

Argumentation is not simply the art of persuasion—it is the architecture of understanding. At the doctoral level, the strength of a student's argument reflects not just their knowledge, but their transformation into a scholar. As chairs, we must move beyond superficial markers of progress—page counts, formatting, checklists—and instead focus on nurturing the student's ability to think, synthesize, and defend with clarity and conviction.

In this chapter, we've examined the foundational elements of strong writing: purpose, coherence, voice, and evidence. We've also acknowledged the modern challenges facing doctoral students—particularly the seduction of generative AI tools that promise quick clarity but often produce shallow mimicry.

Your role is not to police writing, but to protect its integrity.

That means:

- Challenging students to dig deeper when their arguments are too safe.
- Slowing them down when their structure outpaces their synthesis.
- Guiding them to find their own voice—not the voice of AI, or past students, or even their chair.

The dissertation is not a product; it is a process. One that demands critical self-awareness, rhetorical agility, and intellectual courage. These cannot be downloaded. They must be developed with your mentorship as the scaffolding.

So, as you close each writing meeting, ask yourself:

- Did I help this student hear their own thinking more clearly?
- Did I elevate precision over performance?
- Did I reinforce that writing is not just a deliverable—but a demonstration of scholarly becoming?

Because in the end, a dissertation filled with references but devoid of voice is not a contribution—it's a simulation.

Let your students write not just to complete a program—but to claim their place in the scholarly conversation. That is the true goal of Chapter 8. And that is the mark of a transformational chair.

Before You Hit Send: The High-Integrity Feedback Protocol

At the doctoral level, feedback is not commentary. It is intervention.

Every time you return a draft, you are shaping more than sentences—you are shaping confidence, direction, and scholarly identity. Vague feedback slows progress. Overwhelming feedback paralyzes. Tone-deaf feedback erodes trust. Delayed feedback compounds doubt.

Most chairs believe they are rigorous. Fewer ask whether they are clear.

"Needs more development."
"Expand this section."
"Clarify your argument."

These phrases may feel efficient, but they transfer the cognitive burden back to the student without guidance. They create revision cycles instead of progress. They generate anxiety instead of insight.

High-quality doctoral mentorship requires feedback that is:

- Specific
- Prioritized
- Explanatory
- Actionable
- Respectful
- Structured

Rigor is not measured by how many comments you leave. It is measured by whether your comments accelerate learning. Before sending feedback, pause. Audit your response. Ensure that what you are returning to the student is not merely critique—but direction. Not just correction—but development.

This checklist exists to protect the integrity of your mentorship. Use it as a final calibration before you hit send.

Rigor Without Ambiguity: A Chair's Feedback Standard

☐ I identified specific strengths (not just "good job")

☐ I provided page/paragraph references for all critiques

☐ I explained WHY a change is needed, not just WHAT to change

☐ I suggested specific revision strategies or examples

☐ I prioritized feedback (critical vs. minor issues)

☐ I avoided vague terms ("needs more development")

☐ I checked tone for respectful, growth-oriented language

☐ I included next steps and timeline expectations

Evaluating AI-Assisted Work: Preserving Intellectual Ownership

Artificial intelligence is now embedded in the research and writing process. Doctoral candidates may use AI tools for brainstorming, outlining, summarizing literature, refining language, or stress-testing ideas. The question is no longer whether AI will be used. The question is whether it is being used responsibly.

At the doctoral level, authorship is not about who typed the words. It is about who owns the thinking.

When reviewing AI-assisted work, your task is not to police technology. It is to evaluate intellectual contribution. A student may appropriately use AI for ideation or structural assistance while still demonstrating mastery. Conversely, a polished draft may conceal shallow understanding if the student cannot explain or defend its content.

Your role is to distinguish support from substitution.

Clear expectations and consistent review standards prevent both overreaction and negligence. You are not searching for violations; you are verifying scholarship. When AI use is transparent, defensible, and integrated into authentic analysis, it can strengthen learning. When it replaces synthesis, judgment, or methodological reasoning, it undermines doctoral formation.

Use the following checklist to evaluate AI-assisted submissions with clarity and consistency.

Reviewing AI-Assisted Student Work

☐ Student disclosed AI tool usage in accordance with institutional policy

☐ AI usage is appropriate for the task (e.g., ideation, outlining, refinement—not wholesale writing)

☐ Student demonstrates clear understanding of any AI-generated or AI-influenced content

☐ Student can explain and defend AI-influenced claims or arguments

☐ Original intellectual contribution is evident throughout the work

☐ All cited sources have been independently verified (no AI-generated or fabricated references)

☐ Writing reflects the student's authentic scholarly voice

☐ Student substantially revised, critiqued, or enhanced any AI-generated output

Red Flags — Pause and Investigate

☐ Sudden and unexplained shift in writing quality or tone

☐ Citation inconsistencies or unverifiable references

☐ Generic, overly polished, or non-contextualized content

☐ Inability to explain methodology, theory, or findings in the student's own words

☐ Resistance to discussing how the work was produced

Chapter 9 - Argumentation Techniques for Dissertation Writing

Figure 9. [222].

Strong argumentation is at the heart of a compelling dissertation. Doctoral research is not just about presenting data or summarizing existing literature; it is about constructing a logical, well-supported argument that contributes to scholarly discourse. The ability to formulate clear, persuasive arguments is essential for doctoral candidates, as it allows them to position their research within the broader academic landscape, address potential counterarguments, and establish credibility in their field.

Effective argumentation in dissertation writing requires more than just assembling evidence—it involves structuring ideas coherently, using sound reasoning, and integrating supporting research in a meaningful way. Dissertation chairs play a critical role in guiding students through this process, helping them refine their thesis, strengthen their analytical reasoning, and anticipate potential critiques [89]. Understanding the principles of argumentation enables students to develop a dissertation that is not only methodologically sound but also intellectually rigorous and persuasive.

The key aspects of argumentation in dissertation writing include:

- **Structuring an Academic Argument** – A well-organized dissertation follows a logical sequence, where each chapter and section builds upon the previous one. Developing a clear thesis statement, aligning research questions with arguments, and ensuring coherence throughout the dissertation are essential elements of strong argumentation [90].

- **Addressing Counterarguments and Criticism** – Anticipating and responding to potential objections strengthens a dissertation by demonstrating that the researcher has critically engaged with alternative viewpoints and competing theories.

- **Ensuring Coherence and Cohesion in Writing** – Logical flow, well-developed transitions, and thematic consistency help ensure that arguments are presented in a compelling and persuasive manner.

A well-structured dissertation argument provides a solid foundation for engaging in scholarly debate. Strong argumentation techniques not only enhance the clarity and persuasiveness of a dissertation but also prepare students for the peer review process, academic publishing, and professional discourse in their respective fields [91].

This chapter explores the essential principles of argumentation in dissertation writing, offering strategies for developing a compelling research narrative, addressing critiques effectively, and maintaining logical consistency throughout the dissertation. By mastering these techniques, doctoral candidates can elevate the quality of their research and contribute meaningfully to the academic community.

Structuring an Academic Argument

A well-structured academic argument is the foundation of scholarly writing, especially at the doctoral level. It serves as the blueprint guiding the reader through the complexity of your research, enabling them to understand the significance of your findings and how they contribute to the broader field. In this section, we explore the critical components of structuring an academic argument: developing a thesis statement, supporting arguments, and the use of evidence-based argumentation in research.

Developing a Thesis Statement and Supporting Arguments

At the heart of any academic argument lies the thesis statement. The thesis statement is a concise, focused assertion clearly defining the central idea or claim of your research. It tells the reader what you aim to prove or argue and sets the direction for the entire study. Crafting a strong thesis statement requires precision, clarity, and depth, as it serves as the foundation upon which your entire dissertation is built [92].

- **Thesis Development**: The process of developing a thesis begins with identifying a clear research question or problem. Once the problem is defined, the thesis statement must provide a direct response, outlining the main argument or position your research will take. A well-formulated thesis is neither too broad nor too narrow—it must be specific enough to be researchable, yet flexible enough to allow for a nuanced argument [93].

    - **Example of a Thesis Statement**: *This study argues implementing AI-driven tools in supply chain management will significantly improve efficiency, reduce costs, and enhance overall sustainability.*

  This thesis provides a clear, focused argument, which the research will seek to support with evidence and analysis.

- **Supporting Arguments**: Once the thesis statement is in place, the next step is to develop supporting arguments. These are the building blocks of your academic argument. Supporting arguments are the key points reinforcing and expanding upon the thesis. Each supporting argument should provide a clear, logical reason why the thesis is valid, offering evidence, data, or theoretical backing to substantiate the claim [94].

    - **Example**: In the case of the AI in supply chain management thesis, the supporting arguments could include:

        - AI tools reduce human error and increase efficiency in operational processes.

        - AI can optimize inventory management and reduce waste, contributing to cost reduction.

        - AI enhances sustainability by optimizing energy usage and reducing carbon footprints.

Each of these points builds upon the main thesis, reinforcing the argument and contributing to a more comprehensive understanding of the research question.

Using Evidence-Based Argumentation in Research

While a strong thesis statement and supporting arguments are critical, the strength of an academic argument ultimately depends on the quality of evidence supporting it [24]. In doctoral research, arguments must be rooted in credible, robust evidence, which can include empirical data, literature reviews, case studies, or theoretical analysis [95].

- **Evidence-Based Argumentation**: The process of evidence-based argumentation involves presenting data, findings, or scholarly insights substantiating your supporting arguments. Evidence serves as the backbone of your argument, giving it validity and authority [24]. In academic writing, evidence can come from a variety of sources:
    - **Empirical Research**: Data collected through experiments, surveys, or observations provides direct evidence to support claims.
    - **Literature Reviews**: Synthesizing previous research shows how your argument fits within or challenges the existing body of knowledge.
    - **Case Studies**: Real-world examples provide practical evidence to illustrate how your argument applies in specific contexts.
    - **Theoretical Analysis**: Applying or critiquing existing theories gives your argument a solid intellectual foundation.

- **Evaluating and Integrating Evidence**: Simply presenting evidence is not enough; it must be critically evaluated and integrated into your argument. Each piece of evidence should be analyzed to ensure its relevance, reliability, and alignment with the supporting argument. When using evidence, it is important to explain how and why the evidence supports your thesis. This process of linking evidence to your argument strengthens the overall coherence of your work [24].
    - **Example**: If your thesis is about AI in supply chain management, you might provide empirical data showing how specific AI tools have reduced operational costs in companies. This evidence must be contextualized and explained to show how it directly supports your broader argument about AI's benefits.

- **Balancing Evidence and Analysis**: In academic writing, there must be a balance between presenting evidence and offering critical analysis. *Avoid simply listing facts or citing studies without interpretation; instead, integrate the evidence into your argument by analyzing its significance, limitations, and broader implications*. This reflective approach not only strengthens your argument but also demonstrates your ability to engage critically with the material.

o   **Example**: After presenting data on AI's cost-saving potential, you might discuss potential limitations, such as initial implementation costs or the need for employee training, before concluding the long-term benefits outweigh these challenges.

Conclusion

Structuring an academic argument is a process beginning with a clear, focused thesis statement and is built on a series of well-supported arguments. The key to crafting a strong argument lies in the careful use of evidence, which must be integrated with critical analysis to reinforce the central thesis. By mastering the art of structuring academic arguments, doctoral students can ensure their research is not only clear and persuasive but also grounded in robust, evidence-based reasoning. This skill is essential for contributing meaningful insights to the academic community and advancing knowledge in their respective fields.

Addressing Counterarguments

In doctoral research and academic writing, presenting a strong argument is essential, but it is equally important to demonstrate an awareness of opposing viewpoints and effectively address them. Counterarguments—or opposing views—are an inevitable part of scholarly discourse [24]. When writing a dissertation or research paper, acknowledging and refuting counterarguments not only strengthens your position but also shows you have considered the full range of perspectives on the topic. This section explains the process of identifying and refuting opposing viewpoints and how integrating counterarguments can make your overall argument more persuasive and robust.

Identifying and Refuting Opposing Viewpoints

One of the key steps in addressing counterarguments is identifying the opposing viewpoints challenging your thesis or argument. In academic writing, these counterarguments may stem from alternative interpretations of data, competing theories, or critiques of the methods or assumptions underlying your research [24]. _Engaging with these viewpoints demonstrates critical thinking and strengthens your argument by showing you have considered multiple perspectives._

o   **Identifying Counterarguments**: The process begins by thoroughly reviewing the literature, examining opposing theories, and considering potential criticisms of your position. Look for studies or arguments contradicting or challenging your findings or theoretical framework. It is important to approach these opposing views with intellectual openness, as they offer an opportunity to refine and solidify your argument.

   o   **Example**: If your thesis argues artificial intelligence (AI) improves decision- making in supply chain management, a counterargument might suggest reliance on AI reduces human oversight and could lead to systemic errors. This opposing view challenges the assumption that AI always enhances decision-making.

o   **Refuting Counterarguments**: Once opposing viewpoints are identified, the next step is to refute them effectively. Refutation involves presenting evidence or reasoning disproving or weakening the validity of the counterargument. This could include highlighting flaws in the opposing research's methodology, offering counter-evidence contradicting the opposing viewpoint, or demonstrating the counterargument is based on outdated information.

- o **Example**: In response to the counterargument about AI reducing human oversight, you could present evidence showing hybrid models, where AI supports but does not replace human decision-makers, have been shown to improve overall accuracy while maintaining necessary oversight.

The key to refutation is to address opposing viewpoints respectfully and objectively. Rather than dismissing them outright, explain why they are not as convincing as your argument. This balanced approach enhances the credibility of your writing, demonstrating your position holds up under scrutiny.

Strengthening Arguments Through Counterargument Integration

Integrating counterarguments into your research is a powerful strategy for strengthening your overall argument [96]. By engaging with opposing viewpoints rather than ignoring them, you can show your research is comprehensive and your conclusions are more credible because they have withstood critical evaluation.

- **Enhancing Credibility**: When you address counterarguments directly, you show you are not avoiding difficult questions or challenges. This transparency enhances the credibility of your argument because it demonstrates you have thoroughly examined the issue from all angles. *Scholarly research is not about presenting a one-sided argument but rather about engaging in a reasoned, balanced discussion of the evidence*.

  - o **Example**: A researcher writing about the benefits of renewable energy sources could acknowledge the counterargument renewable energy may have high initial costs. However, by addressing this counterargument with data on long-term savings and sustainability benefits, the researcher strengthens their overall argument about a cost-effective renewable energy solution.

- **Demonstrating Mastery of the Field**: Addressing counterarguments also demonstrates a deep understanding of the topic. Scholars who anticipate opposing viewpoints and can offer well-reasoned responses to them show they are well-versed in the literature and complexities of their field [96]. This enhances the quality of the research and positions the writer as a credible and knowledgeable expert.

  - o **Building a More Nuanced Argument**: By incorporating counterarguments, you can build a more nuanced and sophisticated argument. In some cases, engaging with opposing viewpoints may lead to a refinement of your original thesis. Rather than weakening your position, acknowledging the complexity of an issue and addressing counterarguments strengthens your overall argument by making it more comprehensive.

  - o **Example**: If you are writing about the impact of remote work on employee productivity, acknowledging some workers may struggle with isolation or lack of structure in a remote setting allows you to build a more nuanced argument. By addressing these challenges and offering solutions (e.g., regular check-ins or structured schedules), you can create a stronger, more balanced discussion of the benefits and limitations of remote work.

Best Practices for Addressing Counterarguments

To effectively incorporate counterarguments into your academic writing, follow these best practices:

1. **Introduce Counterarguments Fairly**: Present opposing viewpoints clearly and fairly. Avoid misrepresenting or oversimplifying the counterargument, as this can undermine your credibility. Instead, engage with the strongest version of the opposing viewpoint. Ensure logical fallacies are not presented when presenting or evaluating counterarguments.

2. **Use Evidence-Based Refutation**: Refute counterarguments with evidence, whether through empirical data, logical reasoning, or theoretical critique. Make sure your

response is grounded in research rather than relying on opinion or assumptions.

3. **Maintain a Respectful Tone**: When addressing counterarguments, maintain a respectful and objective tone. <u>**Scholarly writing is not adversarial; it is a reasoned discussion**</u>. Engaging with opposing views in a professional and measured way demonstrates your ability to navigate intellectual disagreements constructively.

4. **Link Refutation Back to Your Thesis**: After refuting a counterargument, connect your refutation back to your main thesis or argument. Show the reader how addressing the counterargument reinforces your original position, making it stronger and more comprehensive.

5. **Be Open to Revising Your Argument**: In some cases, addressing counterarguments may reveal weaknesses in your original thesis. Be open to revising your argument in light of new evidence or opposing viewpoints. Scholarly writing is about advancing knowledge, which sometimes means refining or adjusting your position as new information becomes available.

Conclusion

Addressing counterarguments is an essential component of building a strong, persuasive academic argument. By identifying and refuting opposing viewpoints, you demonstrate critical thinking, intellectual openness, and mastery of the subject matter. Moreover, integrating counterarguments into your research strengthens your overall position by showing your argument has withstood critical scrutiny. In doctoral writing, where complexity and nuance are highly valued, engaging with counterarguments not only strengthens your research but also enhances your credibility as a scholar. Through thoughtful and evidence-based refutation, you can present a more balanced, comprehensive, and persuasive argument in your dissertation or research paper.

Coherence and Cohesion in Writing

In academic writing, especially at the doctoral level, coherence and cohesion are essential for effectively communicating complex ideas. These two principles ensure your arguments flow logically, making it easier for your audience to follow and understand your research. Coherence is the logical organization and clarity of ideas, while cohesion connects individual sentences and paragraphs. Together, they contribute to writing being both readable and persuasive, critical qualities for any dissertation or scholarly work [97].

This section explains how to ensure logical flow between arguments and how to write with clarity and purpose for diverse academic and professional audiences.

Ensuring Logical Flow Between Arguments

Coherence in writing means the ideas are logically ordered and connected [98]. It's not enough to simply present facts or findings; those ideas must be organized in a way guiding the reader through your argument, showing how each point builds upon the previous one and leads to a clear conclusion. In doctoral research, where arguments are often complex and multilayered, maintaining coherence is vital to ensure your audience can easily follow the development of your thesis.

- **Structuring Your Argument**: To ensure logical flow, each argument should be carefully structured so it contributes to the overall narrative of your research. Start with a clear thesis statement and ensure each section, paragraph, and sentence connects back to that main argument. Think of your writing as a road map—each point should guide the reader logically to the next.

  - **Example**: If your thesis is about the impact of renewable energy on economic growth, you might first present an overview of the current energy landscape, then discuss the potential benefits of renewable energy, and finally address the economic models predicting growth based on renewable energy investment. Each section should flow logically into the next, building a coherent case for your thesis.

- **Transitioning Between Ideas**: Smooth transitions between ideas and sections are key to maintaining coherence. Transition words and phrases (e.g., therefore, consequently, in contrast, additionally) help signal the relationship between ideas and prevent your writing from feeling disjointed. Use transitions to show cause and effect, contrast different viewpoints, or introduce new supporting evidence.

  - **Example**: After discussing the environmental benefits of renewable energy, you might transition to its economic impact by writing, *"While the environmental advantages are clear, the economic implications of renewable energy adoption are equally significant, as demonstrated by several recent studies."* This sentence links two key aspects of the topic and helps the reader see how the discussion is progressing.

- **Maintaining a Clear Focus**: Coherence is also about staying focused on your central argument. Avoid introducing tangential or unrelated points confusing the reader or disrupting the logical flow of your writing. *Each paragraph should directly contribute to your overall thesis, either by supporting your argument, addressing a counterargument, or presenting evidence.* If a paragraph doesn't contribute to the thesis, it should not be present.

- o **Example**: In a section on the economic benefits of renewable energy, avoid going off-topic by discussing unrelated technologies. Stick to the focus of your argument to maintain coherence.

Writing with Clarity and Purpose for Diverse Audiences

While coherence ensures the logical flow of ideas, cohesion ensures individual sentences and paragraphs are well-connected, contributing to the overall clarity and readability of your writing. Achieving clarity is particularly important in academic writing, where your audience may include experts in your field, interdisciplinary scholars, and even lay readers who may not be as familiar with the technical details of your research.

- o **Clarity in Sentence Structure**: *Writing clearly means crafting sentences easy to read and understand, without unnecessary complexity.* Academic writing often deals with sophisticated ideas, but doesn't mean your sentences should be convoluted. Avoid jargon where possible, or provide clear definitions when technical terms are necessary. *Break down long, complicated sentences into smaller ones to improve readability.*

  - o **Example**: Instead of writing, *"The innovative renewable energy technologies, which have been increasingly adopted due to recent policy changes, are projected to significantly impact global economic models in a manner that suggests potential for long-term growth,"* consider simplifying: *"Recent policy changes have led to the increased adoption of renewable energy technologies. This shift is expected to have a significant impact on global economic growth over the long term."*

- o **Audience Awareness**: When writing for diverse audiences, you must strike a balance between maintaining scholarly rigor and making your work accessible. Consider the needs of your audience. For fellow researchers, technical details and in-depth analysis are expected. However, for interdisciplinary or general audiences, provide context and simplify explanations without losing the essence of your argument. Tailoring your writing for your audience ensures your research is understood and appreciated by all.

  - o **Example**: If your dissertation focuses on highly technical aspects of renewable energy technology, but you anticipate presenting it to a policy-making audience, you might write: *"This technology reduces carbon emissions by 20% compared to traditional methods, providing both environmental and economic benefits. It offers a cost-effective solution for achieving policy targets on climate change."* This version simplifies the technical details while highlighting the relevance for policy discussions.

- o **Purposeful Writing**: Writing with purpose means every sentence and paragraph contributes to your overall research goals. Whether you are introducing new data, analyzing findings, or addressing counterarguments, each part of your writing should serve a clear purpose. Eliminate unnecessary information not directly supporting your argument or advancing your thesis.

- o **Example**: In a section discussing economic models, ensure all supporting data and examples directly tie into your thesis. Avoid including statistics or case studies not contributing to the argument you are making.

- o **Cohesive Paragraphs**: Cohesion within paragraphs is achieved by making sure sentences flow naturally from one to the next [99]. Use topic sentences to introduce the main idea of each paragraph, and ensure the subsequent sentences provide support or elaboration. Avoid abrupt shifts in ideas or topics confusing the reader. Conclude each paragraph with a sentence tying the key point back to the overall argument.

- o **Example**: A well-structured paragraph might begin with a topic sentence like, *"One of the key drivers of economic growth in renewable energy is increased investment in technology."* The following sentences should elaborate on how investment impacts growth, with supporting evidence from research, before concluding with a sentence reinforcing the connection between investment and economic outcomes.

Best Practices for Achieving Coherence and Cohesion

1. **Outline Your Argument**: Before writing, create a detailed outline of your argument, breaking it down into sections and sub-sections. This will help you maintain a clear focus and ensure your ideas are logically organized. Outlines enable your writing to use coherence and cohesion effectively.

2. **Use Transitions Effectively**: Ensure each sentence and paragraph flows smoothly into the next by using appropriate transitions. This prevents your writing from feeling fragmented or disjointed.

3. **Edit for Clarity**: After completing a draft, read through your work to ensure each sentence is clear and concise. Eliminate jargon, redundant phrases, and overly complicated sentence structures.

4. **Revise for Audience**: Keep your audience in mind throughout the writing process. Tailor your language, explanations, and tone to ensure your research is accessible and meaningful to your intended readers.

Conclusion

Coherence and cohesion are essential for producing clear, persuasive, and well-organized academic writing. By ensuring your arguments flow logically and your writing is clear and purposeful, you will engage your audience more effectively and communicate your research in a compelling way. Whether you are addressing fellow scholars, interdisciplinary researchers, or policy-makers, mastering the principles of coherence and cohesion will help you convey complex ideas with clarity and precision, making your work both accessible and impactful.

Building Credible Claims Supported by Evidence

In scholarly writing, particularly at the doctoral level, the ability to construct persuasive and credible arguments is fundamental. This process hinges on transforming simple data into evidence, leveraging logical reasoning to craft compelling claims, and using warrants to connect these claims to your thesis [24]. This section explores the essential components of argumentation and provides a detailed guide for creating robust scholarly arguments.

Key Concepts in Argumentation

A strong argument in academic writing is built on a foundation of well-selected evidence being relevant, high-quality, and logically connected to your claims. Understanding the distinctions between data and evidence, ensuring relevance, and prioritizing data quality are essential steps in constructing compelling arguments [XX24]. This section provides a detailed explanation of these key concepts.

Data vs. Evidence Data/Information

Data refers to basic facts or statements existing independently as factual artifacts. While data serves as a foundation, it holds no inherent argumentative value until it is contextualized. Data is often neutral and descriptive, lacking the interpretive layer needed to form a compelling argument [XX24].

Example:

o   *"The global average temperature has risen by 1.2°C since pre-industrial times."* This is a factual statement presenting data, but it does not, on its own, support a specific claim or thesis.

Evidence

Evidence is data deliberately selected and contextualized to support a claim. When used effectively, evidence becomes the backbone of your argument, aligning directly with your thesis and demonstrating how the data contributes meaningfully to the discussion. Evidence transforms raw data into a persuasive element of your argument by situating it within a logical framework [XX24].

Example:

o   When the fact about the global temperature rise is linked to a claim about the impacts of climate change (e.g., *"The 1.2°C increase in global temperatures since pre-industrial times highlights the urgent need for climate mitigation policies"*), it transitions from data to evidence.

Relevance

The concept of relevance ensures the data or evidence you choose is directly connected to your thesis or argument. Even high-quality data can weaken an argument if it does not contribute meaningfully to the specific claims you are making. Irrelevant data may confuse the reader, dilute the impact of your argument, and distract from your core message [XX24].

To establish relevance:

- Ensure that each piece of evidence directly supports your claims.
- Evaluate whether the evidence advances your broader research goals or thesis.

Example:

If your thesis examines the economic impacts of renewable energy adoption, including data about temperature changes (even if accurate) might be irrelevant unless explicitly tied to the economic argument, such as linking temperature changes to costs of climate mitigation.

Data Quality

The strength and credibility of your argument are directly tied to the quality of the evidence you provide. Quality data is characterized by three critical attributes: *precision, accuracy, and authoritativeness [XX24]*.

Precision

Precision refers to the exactness of measurements or descriptions in the data. It ensures the evidence you use is specific and unambiguous, allowing readers to clearly understand its significance and applicability to your argument.

Example:

- Precise Data: *"The average global temperature in 2023 was 16.9°C, marking a 1.2°C increase since pre-industrial times."*
- Imprecise Data: *"Temperatures have gone up a lot since the industrial revolution."*

  Precise data fosters confidence and clarity, enabling readers to trust the argument

  being made. **Accuracy**

Accuracy involves providing a complete and correct representation of the concepts being studied. Misrepresentation, exaggeration, or selective omission can undermine the credibility of your argument. Accurate data ensures the evidence aligns with established facts and contributes to the argument's validity [XX24].

Example:

- Accurate Data: *"Satellite measurements confirm a 0.13°C increase in average global temperature per decade since 1979."* [100]
- Inaccurate Data: *"Temperatures are increasing at an alarming rate of 5°C per decade."* Accuracy demands rigor in selecting and verifying data to avoid misleading the audience.

Authoritativeness

Authoritative data comes from reliable, credible sources or rigorous methodologies. It reflects sound research practices, such as peer-reviewed studies, government reports, or reputable organizations. Using authoritative data ensures your evidence is grounded in trustworthy information, enhancing your argument's legitimacy [XX24].

Example:

- o Authoritative Data: A report from the *Intergovernmental Panel on Climate Change (IPCC)* on global temperature trends.

- o Non-authoritative Data: An unsourced claim from an anonymous blog.

    Authoritativeness requires critical evaluation of sources to ensure they meet scholarly standards.

Integrating the Key Concepts

To construct a compelling argument:

1. Start by identifying data aligning with your research focus.

2. Transform data into evidence by ensuring it is relevant to your thesis and logically connected to your claims.

3. Evaluate the quality of your data, prioritizing precision, accuracy, and authoritativeness to establish credibility.

4. Avoid including irrelevant or low-quality data weakening your argument.

By adhering to these principles, you create logically sound and persuasive arguments aligned with the rigor of doctoral scholarship.

The Structure of Claims and Warrants

In academic argumentation, claims and warrants form the backbone of persuasive and logical reasoning. This structured approach ensures your arguments are not only clear but also supported by evidence and logical connections. Below, we examine the role of claims and warrants in building compelling arguments and how to use them effectively.

1. **Claims**

A claim is a statement asserting a proposed truth or position central to your argument. It represents the conclusion or idea you want your audience to accept [XX24]. For claims to be persuasive and credible, they must meet specific criteria:

Characteristics of a Credible Claim

Supported by Evidence: A claim must be backed by relevant and high-quality evidence. Evidence transforms a claim from mere opinion into a compelling argument standing up to scrutiny.

Avoids Unsupported Generalizations: Claims must not rely on vague or universally assumed statements like:

- *"Everyone knows that…"*

- *"It is commonly accepted that…"* These types of statements lack substantiation and fail to persuade critical audiences. [See the Logical Fallacies chapter, as well.]

Invalid Claims

Claims unsupported by evidence or relying on personal opinions are inherently weak. They diminish the credibility of your argument and fail to engage a scholarly audience. For example:

- Weak Claim: *"I believe urbanization harms the environment because it feels unnatural."* This claim lacks evidence and is based solely on personal opinion, making it unconvincing.

2. **Warrants**

Warrants are the logical bridges connecting your claims to the evidence provided. They explain *why* the evidence supports the claim and persuade the reader to accept the argument. Without a clear warrant, the relationship between the claim and the evidence may appear disjointed or unconvincing [XX24].

Role of Warrants

- Warrants ensure the evidence provided logically supports the claim.

- They articulate the underlying reasoning linking evidence to the argument.

- By adhering to rules of logic and sound reasoning, warrants provide the necessary foundation for a persuasive argument.

Example of Claims, Evidence, and Warrants

Let's consider a structured argument:

- **Claim**: *"Increased urbanization contributes to climate change."*
  This is the statement proposing a truth or position.

- **Evidence**: *"Studies show urban areas account for 70% of greenhouse gas emissions."*
  This is the relevant data supporting the claim. [101]
- **Warrant**: *"Urbanization concentrates human activity, increasing energy consumption and emissions, thereby driving climate change."*
  The warrant connects the evidence to the claim, explaining how urban areas' high emissions contribute to the broader phenomenon of climate change.

Effective Warrants

Warrants must adhere to principles of logic and sound reasoning. They should:

1. **Be Explicit**: Clearly articulate the reasoning behind the connection between evidence and claim.

2. **Avoid Logical Fallacies**: Ensure the reasoning is free of errors, such as overgeneralizations or false causation.

3. **Strengthen the Argument**: Reinforce the relationship between evidence and claim, persuading the reader of the argument's validity.

Integrating Claims and Warrants

To construct a robust argument:

1. **Begin with a Clear Claim**: Define the central position you are advocating. Ensure it is specific, relevant, and capable of being supported by evidence.

2. **Provide Strong Evidence**: Use high-quality and relevant data to substantiate the claim.

3. **Build Logical Warrants**: Create explicit reasoning connecting the evidence to the claim while ensuring the argument flows logically and persuasively.

By adhering to these principles, you create arguments not only communicating your position effectively but also withstanding critical examination. This structured approach is essential for scholarly discourse, where precision, logic, and clarity are paramount.

The Role of Complex Claims in Doctoral Research

In doctoral research, constructing persuasive and logically sound arguments often requires the use of **complex claims**, which are overarching conclusions supported by multiple interconnected simple claims. This approach ensures each component of the argument is rigorously validated and contributes to the coherence of the overall thesis. The process of building credible complex claims involves a structured methodology integrating evidence, logic, and synthesis [24].

Steps to Construct Credible Complex Claims

When building complex claims, sequence and strategy are paramount to ensuring the complex claims meet required criteria. The following steps provide effective approaches to building acceptable complex claims:

1. **Validate Simple Claims First**

The foundation of a complex claim lies in its constituent simple claims [24]. Each simple claim must:

- Be supported by **high-quality evidence** being relevant, precise, accurate, and authoritative.

- Meet the criteria of **acceptability**, meaning it is free from unsupported generalizations or logical fallacies.

Example of Simple Claims:

- Simple Claim 1: *"Deforestation increases carbon emissions."*

  - Supported by evidence showing cutting down forests releases stored carbon into the atmosphere.

- Simple Claim 2: *"Carbon emissions are a leading cause of global warming."*

- Supported by scientific studies linking greenhouse gas concentrations to rising global temperatures.

By ensuring the credibility of each simple claim individually, you create a solid foundation for building more complex arguments.

2. Develop a Logical Framework

Once the simple claims are validated, they must be logically connected to form a cohesive argument [XX24]. This involves:

- **Creating Warrants**: Logical bridges linking the evidence supporting each simple claim to the overall argument. These warrants must align with the principles of sound reasoning and avoid logical fallacies [XX24].

- **Ensuring Logical Consistency**: The framework should clearly outline how each simple claim contributes to the larger argument, avoiding contradictions or gaps in reasoning [24].

Example of Warrants:

- Warrant 1: *"Deforestation releases carbon dioxide, a greenhouse gas contributing to the atmospheric carbon load."*

- Warrant 2: *"Higher atmospheric carbon levels trap more heat, leading to global warming."*

Together, these warrants establish a logical progression from simple claims to the broader argument.

1. Synthesize into a Major Claim

The final step is to combine the validated simple claims and their logical connections into a **major claim**, which represents the overarching argument or conclusion. This synthesis must demonstrate how the individual claims collectively support the larger thesis [24].

Example of a Major Claim:

- Major Claim: *"Deforestation significantly contributes to global warming."*
  - This major claim draws from the logical integration of:
    - Simple Claim 1 (*"Deforestation increases carbon emissions"*) and
    - Simple Claim 2 (*"Carbon emissions are a leading cause of global warming"*).
  - The synthesis reflects the interdependence of the simple claims and the evidence supporting them.

Practical Applications of Complex Claims in Doctoral Research

Building complex claims in doctoral peer reviewed research is critical. Every dissertation will have a series of simple and complex claims. Warrants and logical bridges are necessary to justify every claim in your dissertation [24]. The next chapter will present the methodology map, which is combined with argumentation and claims to systematically layer and present your theoretical framework selection, problem statement justification, purpose statement justification, significance of study justification, and all of the claims layered together to support your research. The complexity of research is difficult to address, requiring comprehension of requirements and a structured deliberate approach. Every justification and major argument are supported with some key strategies, which are listed below:

1. **Structuring Your Dissertation:**

   - Use simple claims to address specific research questions or hypotheses within individual sections or chapters.

   - Synthesize these claims into a complex claim underpinning the central argument of your dissertation.

2. **Responding to Peer Review:**

   - Demonstrate the validity of your major claim by breaking it down into simple claims and showing how each is supported by evidence and logic.

3. **Building Interdisciplinary Arguments:**

   - In research spanning multiple fields, complex claims allow you to integrate insights from different disciplines into a unified argument.

Benefits of Using Complex Claims

All research will involve one or more complex claims. Our research benefits from the use of complex claims due to:

- **Enhanced Rigor**: Ensures all aspects of your argument are carefully examined and supported.

- **Improved Clarity**: Breaks down large, abstract claims into manageable components, making the argument easier to understand and evaluate.

- **Increased Persuasiveness**: Demonstrates the logical progression from evidence to conclusion, making your argument more compelling to readers.

By mastering the construction of complex claims, you elevate the quality and persuasiveness of your doctoral research, laying the foundation for impactful and defensible scholarship.

Practical Application of Argumentative Frameworks

In scholarly research, particularly in dissertations, the strength of your argument is pivotal to your work's success. Evidence forms the foundation of these arguments, transforming raw data into persuasive insights aligning with your research objectives. A structured approach to building arguments ensures your dissertation achieves both credibility and impact. Below, we explore the practical steps to constructing a robust argumentative framework.

1. Identify Relevant Data

The first step in creating a strong argument is identifying data directly supporting your research questions. This requires:

- **Focusing on Relevance**: Ensure the data you select aligns with the central objectives of your thesis.

- **Avoiding Irrelevance**: Even accurate and high-quality data can detract from your argument if it does not contribute meaningfully to your claims.

Example:

If your dissertation explores the economic benefits of renewable energy, data on global temperature changes—while scientifically accurate—may not be relevant unless connected to economic implications.

2. Assess the Quality of the Data

The credibility of your argument relies on the quality of the data you use. Evaluate your data using three critical criteria:

- **Precision**: Ensure the data includes exact measurements or detailed descriptions, leaving no room for ambiguity.

  - Example: *"Renewable energy investments grew by 15.3% in 2023"* is more precise than *"Renewable energy investments have increased."* [102]

- **Accuracy**: Verify the data provides a correct and comprehensive representation of the concepts being studied, avoiding misrepresentation.

  - Example: Use peer-reviewed studies or official reports to ensure the reliability of your data.

- **Authoritativeness**: Choose data from credible sources such as academic journals, government reports, or respected institutions.

3. Transform Data into Evidence

Data in its raw form lacks the interpretive layer needed to advance your argument. To transform data into evidence:

- **Connect Data to Claims**: Show how the data supports specific statements in your argument.

- **Provide Context**: Explain the significance of the data within the broader scope of your research.

Example:

- Data: *"Solar energy capacity in the U.S. increased by 25% in 2022."* [103]

- Evidence: *"The 25% increase in solar energy capacity in 2022 demonstrates a growing shift towards renewable energy, supporting claims of economic viability and environmental sustainability."*

4. **Develop Logical Warrants**

Warrants are the logical bridges connecting your evidence to your claims. Without warrants, the relationship between your data and your conclusions may appear unclear or unconvincing.

Key Steps:

- Articulate the reasoning behind why the evidence supports the claim.

- Ensure warrants follow logical principles, avoiding fallacies or unsupported assumptions.

Example:

- Claim: *"Increased investment in renewable energy drives job creation."*

- Evidence: *"In 2022, the renewable energy sector created 300,000 new jobs."* [104]

- Warrant: *"Higher investments in renewable energy lead to infrastructure development, which requires additional labor, thereby increasing employment opportunities."*

5. **Build Complex Claims Incrementally**

Dissertations often involve complex claims requiring the integration of multiple simple claims. This process involves:

- **Validating Simple Claims**: Ensure each simple claim is supported by high-quality evidence and logical warrants.

- **Synthesizing Claims**: Combine validated simple claims into a cohesive, overarching argument.

Example:

- Simple Claim 1: *"Deforestation increases carbon emissions."*

- Simple Claim 2: *"Carbon emissions are a leading cause of global warming."*

- Major Claim: *"Deforestation significantly contributes to global warming."*
  This approach allows for a step-by-step validation of the argument, ensuring both clarity and rigor.

Conclusion

By following these structured steps for argumentation, you ensure the arguments in your dissertation are not only credible but also compelling. This systematic approach allows you to:

1. Identify and utilize relevant data effectively.

2. Maintain high standards of quality in your evidence.

3. Construct logical connections between evidence and claims.

4. Build complex arguments that withstand scrutiny.

Implementing these principles enhances the scholarly contribution of your dissertation, paving the way for your readers to accept your work as a significant and impactful addition to the academic field.

Chapter 10 - Redefining the Faculty Role in Dissertation Review Boards

Doctoral education is often described as a rite of passage. But who defines that rite? Who ensures it is built not just on tradition, but on integrity, clarity, and ethical rigor?

The answer lies in part with Dissertation Review Boards—the often-misunderstood guardians of both ethical soundness and academic excellence. These boards, whether Institutional Review Boards (IRBs) or Academic Review Boards (ARBs), serve a vital function in the doctoral ecosystem [105]. And yet, too often, they are treated as bureaucratic hurdles rather than as essential systems of mentorship, quality assurance, and scholarly trust.

As faculty—particularly as dissertation chairs or committee members—we are not bystanders to these processes. We are active participants. More than that, we are interpreters. We translate institutional policy into student understanding. We turn ambiguity into structure. We don't just guide students through the boards—we prepare them to stand confidently before them. Sometimes, the guidance we received as doctoral candidates did not develop us into the fully formed scholars we should be. As a faculty chair, this provides us the opportunity to grow and enhance our scholarly capabilities to ensure we are well formed and supporting our doctoral students as transformational mentors.

Figure 10. [222].

This chapter explores the deeper function of dissertation review boards, reframing them not as punitive checkpoints, but as formative spaces for transformation, and identifies how faculty can serve not as passive enforcers but as co-stewards of scholarly responsibility and excellence.

The Institutional Review Board (IRB):

Ethics as a Practice of Care

The IRB exists to protect those most vulnerable in the research process—human participants. It ensures that every study is conducted with full awareness of potential risks, that those risks are minimized, and that participants are never treated as means to an end.

But in practice, many students experience the IRB as a kind of academic tribunal—slow-moving, opaque, and punitive. This misperception is often exacerbated by unclear faculty guidance, delayed mentorship, or a sense that the IRB's job is to "catch mistakes." [106]

Here's the truth: The IRB is not an obstacle. It is a mirror. It reflects the ethical clarity—or confusion—of the research design. And it calls the student to maturity. Each student is not fully prepared to pass the IRB review by themselves, especially if human subjects are involved. The faculty chair is a critical mentor who brings seasoned experience in research studies to the equation to mentor and support the student, helping ensure their study design and IRB review is effective and efficient [107].

The Chair's Ethical Mandate

As a faculty chair or committee member, your task is not to shortcut the IRB process, nor to turn it into an administrative formality. Your task is to mentor your student into ethical consciousness.

That means:

- Discussing research ethics long before the IRB form is introduced.
- Unpacking concepts like informed consent, coercion, confidentiality, and risk—not as terms to define, but as values to embody.
- Challenging your student to consider the lived experience of their participants and how that shapes risk and respect.
- When lacking, mentor and assist as needed.

Do not assume comprehension. Require demonstration. Ask:

- How will your participants know their rights?
- What happens if someone withdraws from your study?
- Are there risks that go beyond the physical—emotional, cultural, reputational?

Help your student answer these questions not by copying past applications, but by confronting real ethical choices. This is not just about passing a board. It is about building researchers who will carry ethical discernment into every future project.

Mentorship in Action: Structuring IRB Readiness

To ensure readiness and reduce unnecessary IRB delays:

- **Create a pre-IRB checklist** with the student. Include:
    - Clear linkage between research questions and data collection methods.
    - Identification of vulnerable populations and risk mitigations.
    - Language for informed consent that is understandable, accessible, and legally sound.
- **Simulate the IRB process**. Have the student present their ethical plan to you as if defending it before a board. Probe. Push. Invite self-reflection.
- **Use collaborative review tools** (e.g., tracked changes, shared Google Docs) to engage iteratively on IRB applications—not just one final glance before submission.

- **Model how to respond to reviewer comments**. This is a chance to teach not just compliance, but academic diplomacy: clear, respectful, evidence-based response.

Most importantly, help the student see the IRB as an ethics partner, not an obstacle. When they internalize that, they don't just pass the board—they begin to think like scholars of integrity.

IRB Submission Readiness: Compliance Before Collection

No data may be collected until ethical approval is secured. That principle is not procedural formality—it is institutional protection, participant protection, and scholarly integrity.

Too many IRB delays occur not because the study is unethical, but because the application is incomplete, vague, or misaligned with institutional requirements. Missing attachments, outdated training certificates, unclear data security plans, or improperly formatted consent documents can delay approval for weeks—or months. Those delays compound quickly and can destabilize an otherwise well-designed dissertation timeline.

As chair, your role at this stage is not to assume compliance. It is to verify it.

IRB submission should never be exploratory. It should be deliberate, complete, and internally reviewed before entering the formal approval queue. When chairs rigorously pre-review IRB materials, approval cycles shorten, student anxiety decreases, and institutional confidence increases.

Use the following checklist as a pre-submission audit. If any element is incomplete, submission should pause until corrected.

IRB Application Completeness Checklist

☐ Protocol narrative addresses all required institutional elements

☐ Informed consent form uses approved institutional template

☐ Recruitment materials attached and compliant

☐ Data collection instruments included (surveys, interview guides, etc.)

☐ Data security and storage plan clearly detailed

☐ CITI (or equivalent) training certificates current

☐ Chair/advisor reviewed and approved submission

☐ Research timeline feasible and aligned with study scope

☐ Budget and participant compensation clearly explained (if applicable)

The Academic Review Board (ARB):

Beyond Approval—Toward Scholarly Maturity

If the IRB is about protection, the ARB is about precision. It ensures that the dissertation meets the standards of the discipline—not just in content, but in logic, argumentation, coherence, and scholarly voice [108].

Unfortunately, many students are taught to view ARB review as a final hoop—to be cleared with quick edits and a sigh of relief. But the ARB, when functioning well, does more than verify formatting [109]. It asks the deeper questions:

- Does the argument hold?
- Is the logic defensible?
- Has the student mastered—not just mimicked—the scholarly conversation?

The faculty's role is to prepare students not just to write well—but to think, reason, and defend their work with clarity and precision.

Preparing for the Academic Review

Here are practical ways you can prepare your student to meet and exceed ARB expectations:

1. Structure the Feedback Process

- Use milestone-based feedback—chapter by chapter, theme by theme.
- Incorporate structured review forms that include logic, coherence, citation integration, and argument clarity—not just grammar.

2. Teach Argumentation as a Craft

- Break down the parts of a sound argument: claim, warrant, evidence, counterargument.
- Ask: *What are you actually trying to prove—and why does it matter?*

3. Use Defense-Readiness Sessions

- Before ARB submission, hold "mini-defense" sessions.
- Ask students to verbally walk through their methodology, data analysis, and interpretation.
- If they can't explain it clearly, they are not ready.

4. Leverage Writing Tools Judiciously

- Encourage revision tools (e.g., Grammarly, Hemingway Editor) to polish language—but emphasize that no AI can replace scholarly reasoning.
- Remind students: clear writing is the evidence of clear thinking.

ARB Approval: Academic Authorization Before Ethical Submission

Before a study reaches the Institutional Review Board, it must first withstand academic scrutiny. The Academic Review Board (ARB), proposal committee, or equivalent institutional body evaluates something different from IRB compliance. It evaluates intellectual coherence.

The ARB does not primarily assess consent language or data storage plans. It evaluates:

- Whether the problem warrants investigation.

- Whether the literature justifies the study.

- Whether the theoretical framework is defensible.

- Whether the methodology answers the research questions.

If IRB approval protects participants, ARB approval protects scholarship.

Many IRB delays originate upstream—from poorly aligned proposals, unclear frameworks, or insufficient literature grounding. When the proposal lacks structural integrity, ethical review becomes secondary because the design itself is unstable.

As chair, your responsibility is to ensure that the proposal is not merely formatted correctly—but intellectually defensible.

Use this checklist to verify that the study is academically ready for institutional authorization before it proceeds to ethical review or data collection.

ARB Readiness Checklist

☐ Proposal follows institutional template exactly

☐ Problem–purpose–method alignment is explicit

☐ Literature review demonstrates gap and contribution

☐ Theoretical framework is clearly identified and justified

☐ Methodology is rigorous and appropriate to research questions

☐ All committee members have formally approved the proposal

☐ Student can defend all methodological choices without reliance on notes

Reframing Review Boards: From Bureaucracy to Stewardship

When faculty distance themselves from the review board process—or treat it as "someone else's job"—they forfeit a vital opportunity. These boards are not punitive systems. They are mentorship systems at scale.

Your engagement as a chair shape how the student sees these reviews:

- As growth, not gatekeeping.
- As dialogue, not decree.
- As accountability, not antagonism.

We must stop reinforcing the myth that academic rigor is synonymous with unnecessary delay or cold detachment. Rigor is not about withholding support—it's about raising standards through intentional structure and compassionate challenge [110].

Final Reflection: Standing Watch with Wisdom

Serving on or preparing a student for a dissertation review board is a sacred trust. You are standing at the intersection of ethics and excellence. The final guardian of both.

But you are not there to defend tradition. You are there to defend the *purpose* of scholarship itself.

Ask yourself:

- Am I preparing students to face these boards with clarity and confidence?
- Have I taught them not just to pass—but to embody the values of ethical, rigorous research?
- Do I treat these reviews as hoops, or as hallowed ground?

If you can answer yes, then you are not simply overseeing a process.
You are cultivating a generation of scholars who will write, research, and lead with conscience.

Because in the end, the review boards do not exist to say *yes* or *no*—they exist to ensure that when the answer is yes, it is earned with honor.

Conclusion

The review boards—IRB and ARB alike—are not adversaries in the doctoral process. They are stewards of ethics, quality, and clarity. But whether they function as mechanisms of mentorship or mechanisms of obstruction depends largely on us—the faculty who prepare students to meet them, speak to them, and learn from them.

Too often, faculty treat these boards as external checkpoints, something to be endured or avoided. But the truth is this: if a student walks into the review process unprepared, confused, or afraid, it is not a failure of the student—it is a failure of their guidance [111].

Faculty must reclaim our role—not as passive advisors, but as ethical architects. Our work is not to "get them through" these committees. Our work is to ensure that when they arrive, they do so with intellectual integrity, ethical clarity, and scholarly courage.

That means:

- Teaching ethical discernment—not just form completion.
- Requiring clarity of argument—not just compliance with formatting.
- Modeling a collaborative tone with institutional boards—not a defensive one.

The review boards are not the enemy. They are the final crucible where theory meets consequence, where abstraction becomes accountability. And when faculty rise to this moment—mentoring not with avoidance, but with intention—we don't just graduate students. We graduate scholars worthy of the title.

Let us stop fearing the boards.
Let us shape students who are ready to lead through them.

Chapter 11 - Preparing for the Dissertation Defense

Figure 11. [222].

The dissertation defense is the culmination of years of rigorous research, critical thinking, and academic perseverance. It represents the final step in the doctoral journey, where candidates must demonstrate mastery of their research topic, defend their methodology and findings, and engage in scholarly dialogue with their dissertation committee. Preparing for this milestone requires not only a thorough understanding of the research but also strong presentation skills, strategic preparation, and the ability to respond confidently to committee questions and critiques.

A successful dissertation defense requires careful planning, clear communication, and a structured approach to addressing potential challenges. The defense is not merely an evaluation of the dissertation itself; it is an opportunity for students to showcase their expertise, articulate the significance of their research, and establish themselves as scholars in their respective fields. The dissertation chair plays a critical role in preparing students for this event, guiding them through the process of refining their presentation, anticipating committee concerns, and developing strategies for responding to questions effectively [112].

The key aspects of dissertation defense preparation include:

- **Strategies for Defense Preparation and Presentation Coaching** – Developing a structured defense presentation, practicing delivery, and refining key arguments ensure that candidates present their research confidently and effectively.

- **Managing Committee Dynamics and Candidate Readiness** – Understanding the expectations of dissertation committee members, preparing for potential critiques, and navigating the defense discussion with professionalism and poise are essential for a smooth defense experience.

- **Assessing Defense Performance and Guiding Final Revisions** – Following the defense, students must incorporate committee feedback, make necessary revisions, and ensure their dissertation meets institutional requirements for final submission.

The dissertation defense is often perceived as an intimidating process, but with proper preparation and support, students can approach it as a rewarding academic experience [113]. Faculty mentors and dissertation chairs must equip students with the skills and confidence to articulate their research clearly, defend their conclusions with evidence, and engage in intellectual discourse that reflects their growth as scholars [114].

This chapter provides a comprehensive guide to preparing for the dissertation defense, offering practical strategies for refining presentations, addressing committee feedback, and ensuring students are ready to succeed in their final academic milestone. By fostering a culture of preparation, confidence, and scholarly excellence, dissertation chairs can help students navigate the defense process with clarity and poise, setting the stage for their transition into the next phase of their academic or professional careers.

Strategies for Defense Preparation and Presentation Coaching

The dissertation defense represents the culmination of a doctoral candidate's research journey, serving as both a rigorous academic examination and an opportunity to showcase the significance of their work. Effective preparation is crucial for ensuring confidence, clarity, and the ability to engage with the dissertation committee in a compelling manner.

Key strategies for defense preparation include:

- **Developing a Clear and Structured Presentation:** Candidates should create a well-organized presentation that highlights the research problem, theoretical framework, methodology, findings, and contributions to the field. The presentation should be logically structured, engaging, and concise.

- **Practicing Delivery with Faculty and Peers:** Rehearsing the defense in front of faculty members, mentors, and fellow students can provide valuable feedback and help candidates refine their presentation skills.

- **Anticipating and Preparing for Questions:** Candidates should compile a list of potential questions based on their dissertation's strengths, weaknesses, and potential areas of scrutiny. Practicing responses to these questions fosters confidence and readiness for the defense.

- **Using Visual Aids Effectively:** Charts, graphs, and key slides should enhance, rather than overshadow, the oral presentation. Avoiding excessive text and focusing on clear, impactful visuals ensures a more engaging presentation.

- **Managing Time Efficiently:** The presentation should be carefully timed to adhere to the institution's requirements, allowing sufficient time for discussion and committee questions.

- **Building Confidence Through Mock Defenses:** Simulating the defense environment through structured mock sessions can help candidates refine their delivery, identify weak areas, and develop strategies for responding to challenging inquiries [115].

By integrating these strategies, dissertation candidates can approach their defense with clarity, preparedness, and the ability to effectively communicate the impact of their research.

Managing Committee Dynamics and Candidate Readiness

Navigating the interpersonal dynamics of the dissertation committee is a crucial aspect of a successful defense [116]. Dissertation chairs play an essential role in preparing candidates for these interactions and ensuring that committee expectations are met [117].

Key considerations for managing committee dynamics include:

- **Understanding Committee Expectations:** Candidates should be well-informed about the committee members' academic interests, perspectives, and areas of expertise to anticipate possible lines of questioning.

- **Encouraging Professional and Respectful Engagement:** Maintaining a respectful and open-minded approach during the defense fosters constructive dialogue and demonstrates academic maturity.

- **Addressing Committee Feedback Proactively:** Candidates should be prepared to acknowledge and respond to constructive criticism, demonstrating their ability to engage in scholarly discourse.

- **Ensuring Emotional and Intellectual Readiness:** Dissertation chairs should assess whether the candidate is fully prepared for the defense, both academically and psychologically, providing reassurance and strategies for managing anxiety.

- **Facilitating Constructive Pre-Defense Meetings:** Holding pre-defense meetings with committee members allows candidates to gain insight into key concerns and refine their arguments accordingly.

- **Encouraging Adaptability in Response to Committee Queries:** Candidates should be flexible in their responses, acknowledging areas for improvement while confidently defending their research choices.

By understanding and effectively managing committee dynamics, candidates can navigate their dissertation defense with professionalism, composure, and intellectual agility.

Assessing Defense Performance and Guiding Final Revisions

Following the defense, dissertation chairs must provide structured guidance to help candidates refine their research based on committee feedback [118]. This phase ensures that the final dissertation meets institutional standards and academic rigor.

Key aspects of assessing defense performance include:

- **Evaluating Presentation Effectiveness:** Committee members assess how well the candidate articulated key arguments, addressed questions, and maintained clarity in their delivery.

- **Reviewing Committee Feedback:** Dissertation chairs should help candidates categorize committee feedback into major revisions, minor refinements, and editorial suggestions to prioritize post-defense improvements.

- **Ensuring Alignment with Research Objectives:** Any revisions should align with the study's original objectives while addressing gaps or concerns raised during the defense.

- **Establishing a Clear Revision Timeline:** Providing a structured timeline for incorporating revisions ensures that candidates meet final submission deadlines efficiently.

- **Conducting a Post-Defense Debrief:** Chairs should schedule a meeting with candidates to discuss defense strengths, areas for improvement, and final dissertation expectations.

- **Finalizing the Dissertation for Institutional Approval:** Ensuring that formatting, citations, and structural integrity align with institutional guidelines is a critical final step before submission [119].

By effectively assessing defense performance and guiding final revisions, dissertation chairs can support candidates in completing their research with scholarly excellence and confidence in their contributions to their field.

Conclusion

Preparing for the dissertation defense requires a multifaceted approach that encompasses structured preparation, effective presentation skills, committee engagement, and post-defense refinement. Through meticulous guidance, strategic rehearsal, and a clear understanding of committee expectations, candidates can approach their defense with confidence and professionalism. Dissertation chairs play an instrumental role in ensuring that doctoral candidates not only defend their research successfully but also leave a lasting scholarly impact within their discipline.

Defense Readiness Protocol: The Final Two-Week Calibration

The dissertation defense is not a ceremony. It is an examination of intellectual ownership.

By the time a candidate reaches this stage, the research should be complete, the argument defensible, and the methodology coherent. The defense is not the moment to discover structural weaknesses, unresolved committee concerns, or logistical confusion. It is the moment to demonstrate mastery.

Most defense failures are not the result of poor scholarship. They are the result of poor preparation. Late draft circulation creates committee frustration. Unrehearsed presentations expose avoidable weaknesses. Unanticipated questions reveal gaps in conceptual clarity. Unclear revision expectations generate post-defense conflict.

The final two weeks before defense are not for rewriting the dissertation. They are for stabilizing the event.

As chair, you are responsible for ensuring three forms of readiness:

1. Administrative stability

2. Scholarly defensibility
3. Committee alignment

If any one of these is weak, the defense becomes unpredictable.

The following checklist is a structured audit for the final two weeks. It ensures that the candidate is not merely hoping to pass—but prepared to defend.

Two Weeks Before Defense: Readiness Checklist

☐ Student has circulated final draft to full committee

☐ All committee members confirmed attendance

☐ Defense logistics confirmed (room, technology, format)

☐ Student has prepared 20–30 minute overview presentation

☐ Mock defense conducted with feedback incorporated

☐ Student can articulate study limitations and implications

☐ Student prepared responses to anticipated questions

☐ Committee members submitted preliminary questions/concerns

☐ Student understands post-defense revision process

Section 3: Best Practices for Effective Dissertation Leadership

Strong doctoral relationships are forged not only through empathy and encouragement, but through shared clarity of purpose. In Section 2, we explored the emotional intelligence and ethical awareness required to mentor with humanity—to build trust, recognize diversity of experience, and establish a mentorship alliance rooted in mutual respect.

But even the most supportive relationship cannot substitute for structure.

A great chair is not only a guide in moments of struggle—but also an architect of progress. Students thrive when the path ahead is visible, when ambiguity is reduced, and when milestones feel like attainable steps rather than looming cliffs. This is especially critical in doctoral education, where timelines stretch over years, feedback cycles are slow, and imposter syndrome often thrives in the shadows of uncertainty [120].

It is in this space—between encouragement and expectation—that structure becomes liberation.

Figure S3. [222].

Section 3 will equip you with the tools to transform your mentorship from responsive to proactive. You'll learn how to frame the dissertation journey with clarity, define key milestones with purpose, and prevent stagnation through intentional pacing and measurable checkpoints.

Because relationships without structure create dependency.
And structure without relationship breeds detachment.

But when both exist—when trust meets trajectory—the master key unlocks the vault of transformation.

Chapter 12 - The Role of Peer Review in Dissertation Supervision

Figure 12. [222].

Peer review serves as a cornerstone of academic integrity, ensuring the quality, validity, and originality of scholarly research [121]. Within the realm of doctoral research, peer review acts as both a gatekeeping mechanism and a developmental tool, fostering rigorous academic discourse while refining the research process [122]. This chapter explores the critical role of peer review in dissertation supervision, highlighting its key functions, methodologies, and benefits for doctoral candidates.

At its core, peer review is the process by which experts in a given field evaluate a manuscript to assess its contribution, accuracy, and alignment with academic standards. According to Elsevier, one of the leading academic publishers, the primary components of peer review include:

• **Evaluation by Experts** – Manuscripts are reviewed by independent scholars with expertise in the subject area to ensure methodological soundness and originality.

• **Confidentiality** – The process is conducted with strict confidentiality to protect intellectual property and the integrity of scholarly evaluation.

• **Constructive Feedback** – Reviewers provide detailed critiques, offering suggestions to enhance the quality and impact of the research.

• **Editorial Decision-Making** – Journal editors or dissertation committees use peer evaluations to determine whether a work should be accepted, revised, or rejected.

• **Integrity and Objectivity** – The process is structured to be impartial, ensuring that biases do not influence academic assessments.

In the context of doctoral research, integrating peer review into dissertation supervision offers numerous advantages. By engaging in structured peer evaluations, students refine their ability to analyze research critically, address methodological concerns, and articulate their arguments effectively. Peer review fosters resilience, as students learn to navigate critiques and improve their work based on scholarly discourse. Furthermore, it prepares them for the broader academic publishing process, equipping them with the skills needed to submit research to peer-reviewed journals and conferences.

This chapter will explore the essential components of peer review in dissertation supervision, examining best practices for integrating peer feedback into the research process, guiding students in providing and receiving critiques, and leveraging peer review as a means of enhancing scholarly rigor. Through a structured approach, faculty can support doctoral candidates in developing high-quality dissertations that contribute meaningfully to their academic disciplines.

Importance of Peer Review in Scholarly Research

Peer review serves as a fundamental pillar of scholarly research, ensuring that academic work adheres to rigorous standards of quality, credibility, and intellectual integrity [123]. In the context of dissertation supervision, integrating peer review fosters an environment of scholarly discourse, providing doctoral candidates with opportunities to refine their arguments, address potential weaknesses, and strengthen the overall validity of their research.

The value of peer review lies in its ability to expose research to multiple perspectives, encouraging critical engagement with methodologies, theoretical frameworks, and empirical findings [124]. By undergoing structured peer evaluations, students learn to:

- **Enhance their analytical skills** by critically assessing scholarly work, both their own and that of their peers.

- **Identify gaps and weaknesses** in their research through constructive feedback.

- **Develop resilience and adaptability** by engaging in scholarly dialogue and revising their work in response to critiques.

- **Improve clarity and coherence** in their writing by receiving feedback on argumentation, structure, and logical consistency [125].

Dissertation chairs should emphasize that peer review is not merely a corrective mechanism but a crucial part of the scholarly research process that cultivates a culture of academic excellence and collaboration.

Encouraging Students to Engage in Peer Review Early in Their Program

Introducing doctoral students to peer review early in their academic journey provides them with essential skills for evaluating scholarly work and integrating feedback effectively [126]. Encouraging engagement in peer review throughout the dissertation process offers several benefits:

- **Fostering a collaborative research culture:** Students gain exposure to different research methodologies, theories, and analytical perspectives, enriching their own work.

- **Developing constructive critique skills:** The ability to provide and receive scholarly feedback prepares students for the review process in academic publishing.

- **Reducing isolation in the dissertation journey:** Regular interaction with peers fosters a sense of community, mitigating the often-solitary nature of doctoral research.

- **Enhancing preparation for journal submission:** Engaging in structured peer review helps students understand the expectations of scholarly publication, increasing their chances of successful submissions [127].

To institutionalize peer review within dissertation supervision, chairs can:

- **Encourage participation in writing groups:** Creating peer-led dissertation writing groups fosters accountability and sustained engagement with research development.

- **Facilitate structured peer review workshops:** Organizing periodic peer feedback sessions helps students systematically refine their work before submitting to their committees.

- **Promote engagement with academic conferences:** Encouraging students to present research at conferences exposes them to informal peer review through scholarly discussions and feedback.

By integrating peer review into early stages of dissertation research, students become more adept at refining their arguments, defending their methodologies, and engaging in intellectual discourse that strengthens their overall research trajectory [128].

Integrating Peer Review into Dissertation Committee Evaluations

Dissertation committees play a pivotal role in assessing and guiding doctoral research, and incorporating peer review as part of committee evaluations can enhance both the quality and effectiveness of feedback [129]. A structured approach to integrating peer review within the dissertation evaluation process includes:

1. **Formal Peer Review Before Committee Submission:** Encouraging students to seek feedback from peers before submitting drafts to the committee can lead to higher-quality submissions, reducing extensive revisions at later stages.

2. **Incorporating Peer Review Assessments into Committee Meetings:** Structuring committee discussions to include insights from peer feedback sessions ensures that student research has been critically evaluated from multiple perspectives before formal assessments.

3. **Using Peer Review as a Training Mechanism:** Teaching students to engage with and apply peer review feedback strengthens their ability to revise their dissertation in alignment with scholarly standards.

4. **Encouraging Cross-Committee Peer Review:** Allowing students from different dissertation committees to review each other's work expands their exposure to diverse disciplinary perspectives and enhances interdisciplinary dialogue.

By institutionalizing peer review within the dissertation committee framework, students gain a more comprehensive understanding of their research's strengths and weaknesses before final submission. Furthermore, this approach aligns with best practices in scholarly research, preparing doctoral candidates for their future roles as academic professionals and contributing scholars [130].

Conclusion

The role of peer review in dissertation supervision is multifaceted, serving as both a quality control mechanism and an essential skill-building tool for doctoral candidates. By encouraging students to engage in peer review early in their program, fostering a culture of collaborative critique, and integrating peer evaluations into dissertation committee assessments, chairs can ensure that students develop into rigorous, well-prepared scholars. Through this structured engagement with peer feedback, doctoral candidates not only enhance the quality of their dissertation but also acquire the critical evaluative skills necessary for a successful academic career.

Chapter 13 - Key Principles of Effective and Professional Peer Review

Peer review is the backbone of academic credibility, ensuring that scholarly research meets the highest standards of quality, validity, and ethical rigor [131]. Within the doctoral research process, peer review serves a dual role: it acts as a quality assurance mechanism while also fostering a culture of constructive critique and intellectual refinement [132]. By engaging in peer review, both reviewers and authors participate in a dynamic scholarly dialogue, enhancing the clarity, coherence, and impact of research contributions.

The fundamental purpose of peer review is to provide an objective assessment of a manuscript's strengths and weaknesses. According to Elsevier and other leading academic institutions, the essential components of effective peer review include:

Figure 13. [222].

- **Maintaining Objectivity and Fairness** – Evaluations must be based solely on the merits of the research, free from personal biases, conflicts of interest, or preferential treatment.

- **Providing Constructive and Actionable Feedback** – Rather than simply identifying flaws, peer reviewers should offer precise suggestions that enable authors to refine their work and improve clarity and argumentation.

- **Following a Structured Review Approach** – A thorough review requires systematic assessment, examining elements such as research design, methodology, argumentation, and adherence to ethical research practices.

- **Balancing Positive and Critical Feedback** – Effective peer review highlights both the strengths and areas for improvement, ensuring that critiques are constructive and facilitate scholarly development.

The peer review process in doctoral research is not merely a procedural requirement; it is an essential component of academic training. Doctoral students who engage in peer review develop critical analytical skills, learning to assess the validity of research arguments, identify gaps in methodology, and synthesize existing knowledge with their own contributions [133]. Moreover, engaging in structured peer evaluations helps students prepare for the challenges of the academic publishing process, where rigorous peer review is the norm [134].

This chapter explores the key principles of professional peer review, offering faculty guidance on mentoring students in both conducting and responding to reviews. Topics covered include strategies for ensuring objectivity, methods for delivering constructive critiques, and techniques for structuring evaluations to maximize impact. By mastering the principles of professional peer review, doctoral candidates not only strengthen their dissertations but also cultivate a scholarly mindset that will serve them throughout their academic and professional careers.

Maintaining Objectivity and Fairness

Peer review serves as a fundamental mechanism in ensuring academic rigor, integrity, and quality within scholarly research [135]. To uphold its credibility, reviewers must maintain objectivity and fairness, ensuring that their evaluations are grounded in scholarly principles rather than personal biases or preferences.

Focusing on Research Content Rather than Personal Opinions

A hallmark of effective peer review is the ability to separate personal opinions from academic evaluation [136]. Reviewers should:

- Assess research based on its merit, coherence, and contribution to the field rather than subjective preferences.

- Remain neutral regarding the author's background, institution, or theoretical stance.

- Avoid making judgments based on disciplinary or methodological biases, instead ensuring that critiques are evidence-based and academically justified.

Applying Consistent Standards Across All Reviews

Fairness in peer review requires uniform application of evaluative criteria [137]. Reviewers should:

- Establish clear, standardized criteria for assessing research quality, including clarity of argument, methodological rigor, and originality.

- Ensure that the same level of scrutiny is applied to all submissions, preventing preferential treatment or undue criticism.

- Recognize and mitigate unconscious biases that may influence their assessments.

By maintaining these principles, reviewers help foster an equitable and academically rigorous peer review process that enhances the credibility and reliability of scholarly research.

Providing Constructive and Actionable Feedback

A well-executed peer review not only identifies areas for improvement but also provides meaningful guidance that authors can use to refine their work [138]. Constructive feedback should be precise, practical, and professionally framed.

Offering Specific Suggestions Rather than Vague Critiques

Generic critiques such as "this section is unclear" or "the argument is weak" provide little value to the author. Instead, reviewers should:

- Identify specific passages where clarity is lacking and suggest ways to improve them.

- Point out areas where evidence is insufficient and recommend additional sources or data.

- Highlight structural weaknesses and propose strategies for improving logical progression and coherence.

Framing Critiques in a Professional Tone

The effectiveness of peer review feedback is largely determined by its tone and delivery [139]. Reviewers should:

- Use a respectful and collegial tone, recognizing the effort and intellectual investment of the author.

- Avoid dismissive or overly harsh language that may discourage constructive revision.

- Frame critiques as opportunities for improvement rather than as definitive judgments on research quality.

By ensuring that feedback is both actionable and professional, reviewers contribute to a productive scholarly discourse that fosters academic growth and research refinement.

Following a Structured Review Approach

A systematic review process ensures that evaluations are thorough, comprehensive, and well-balanced [140]. A structured approach allows reviewers to assess research consistently and provide meaningful feedback.

Assessing Clarity of Research Questions and Objectives

One of the primary responsibilities of a reviewer is to determine whether the research questions and objectives are clearly defined and appropriately framed [141]. Key considerations include:

- Are the research questions specific, measurable, and aligned with the study's objectives?

- Do the objectives clearly articulate the study's intended contributions?

- Are key concepts and terms adequately defined?

Evaluating Argumentation, Methodology, and Logical Flow

Beyond research questions, reviewers should critically assess the logical structure and methodological integrity of the study [142]. This includes:

- Examining the coherence of the argument and its alignment with existing literature.

- Assessing the appropriateness and execution of the research methodology.

- Evaluating whether the study's conclusions logically follow from the data and analysis.

By following a structured review approach, reviewers ensure that their evaluations are consistent, methodical, and conducive to the author's scholarly development.

Balancing Positive and Critical Feedback

Effective peer review is not solely about identifying flaws; it also involves recognizing and reinforcing the strengths of the research [143]. A balanced review fosters motivation and encourages meaningful revisions.

Highlighting Strengths Alongside Areas for Improvement

A comprehensive peer review acknowledges well-executed aspects of the research while also providing constructive criticism. Reviewers should:

- Identify and commend well-articulated arguments, methodological rigor, or innovative contributions.

- Highlight aspects that enhance the research's clarity, coherence, and scholarly impact.

- Provide a balanced assessment that encourages refinement without undermining the author's confidence.

Promoting Argument Coherence and Research Significance

Ultimately, the goal of peer review is to enhance the quality of academic discourse [144]. Reviewers should:

- Ensure that suggested revisions improve the overall coherence and persuasiveness of the research.

- Encourage the author to position their study within the broader scholarly landscape, reinforcing its significance and contributions.

- Guide the author toward strengthening their research's impact while maintaining their unique scholarly voice.

By integrating positive reinforcement with constructive critique, peer reviewers play a crucial role in shaping high-quality research and advancing academic knowledge.

Conclusion

The principles of effective and professional peer review revolve around objectivity, fairness, constructive feedback, structured assessment, and a balanced approach to critique. By upholding these principles, reviewers not only contribute to the integrity of academic research but also support the development of scholars in producing meaningful, impactful work. When peer review is conducted with rigor and professionalism, it becomes a powerful mechanism for maintaining the highest standards of research excellence.

Chapter 14 - Communication Strategies for Chairs and Committees

Figure 14. [222].

Effective communication is the foundation of successful dissertation supervision, playing a critical role in guiding doctoral candidates through the research process. Dissertation chairs and committee members must maintain clear, structured, and transparent communication to ensure that students receive timely guidance, constructive feedback, and the support necessary to complete their research successfully. Without well-defined communication strategies, misunderstandings can arise, delaying progress, increasing frustration, and undermining the mentorship process.

Doctoral research is a complex and iterative process that requires frequent interaction between students, faculty mentors, and dissertation committees. Each stage of dissertation development—from proposal formulation to the final defense—demands precise and structured communication to align expectations, address challenges, and refine the student's research. Dissertation chairs serve as the primary point of contact, facilitating discussions between students and committee members, resolving conflicts, and ensuring that the dissertation process remains productive and academically rigorous.

The key aspects of effective communication in dissertation supervision include:

- **Fostering Productive Dialogue and Resolving Conflicts** – Open, transparent discussions help mitigate potential misunderstandings and prevent conflicts from escalating. Faculty must create an environment where students feel comfortable asking questions, seeking clarification, and engaging in academic discussions.

- **Setting Clear Expectations for Student and Committee Collaboration** – Establishing structured timelines, feedback mechanisms, and milestone checkpoints ensures that all parties remain aligned in terms of research goals and dissertation requirements.

- **Managing Difficult Conversations and Handling Student Concerns** – Faculty must be prepared to navigate challenging discussions related to research setbacks, revisions, or personal struggles that may impact a student's progress. A balanced approach that incorporates empathy, professionalism, and academic rigor is essential.

Strong communication strategies are not only beneficial for students but also contribute to a more cohesive and effective dissertation committee. Clear and well-structured interactions between committee members help maintain consistency in feedback, prevent conflicting guidance, and uphold academic standards. Moreover, establishing effective communication norms allows faculty to provide constructive criticism while fostering a supportive and encouraging research environment.

This chapter provides a comprehensive exploration of best practices for communication in dissertation supervision. It examines strategies for facilitating clear and consistent interactions, resolving conflicts, and handling difficult conversations with professionalism and sensitivity. By mastering these communication techniques, dissertation chairs and committee members can enhance the dissertation experience, ensuring that students remain engaged, motivated, and on track for academic success.

Fostering Productive Dialogue and Resolving Conflicts

Effective dissertation leadership is built on clear, constructive, and transparent communication among dissertation chairs, committee members, and doctoral candidates. The dissertation process is an intricate academic journey that requires continuous dialogue, negotiation, and critical feedback. Ensuring that these interactions remain productive, professional, and solution-focused is essential for both student success and maintaining a collaborative academic environment.

Dissertation chairs must set the tone and expectations for all communication, modeling respect, professionalism, and academic rigor in their interactions. Beyond simply facilitating discussions, chairs play a crucial role in mediating conflicts, aligning committee feedback, and empowering students to engage with scholarly critique in a way that strengthens their work rather than discouraging progress.

This section explores key strategies for fostering productive dialogue and resolving conflicts among students, committee members, and chairs. By employing active listening techniques, structured conflict resolution methods, and diplomatic leadership, dissertation chairs can prevent misunderstandings, maintain professional discourse, and keep the research process moving forward smoothly.

1. Establishing a Culture of Respect and Professionalism

The foundation of productive dialogue in the dissertation process is built upon mutual respect, professional engagement, and shared academic goals. Dissertation chairs must proactively cultivate an environment where students and committee members feel heard, valued, and able to express concerns without fear of judgment or retaliation.

Setting Communication Expectations from the Outset

Early in the dissertation process, chairs should establish clear communication norms by outlining expectations for:

- **Professionalism in feedback delivery:** Emphasizing that critique should be constructive, specific, and oriented toward strengthening the student's research.

- **Tone and approach in discussions:** Ensuring that interactions remain academic rather than personal, even when disagreements arise.

- **Respecting different perspectives:** Recognizing that committee members may approach research from diverse theoretical or methodological standpoints, and students may require guidance in navigating conflicting feedback.

- **Timely and clear responses:** Encouraging committee members and students to communicate in a timely and structured manner to avoid last-minute confusion or misalignment.

A formalized Dissertation Agreement or Memorandum of Understanding (MOU) can be useful in codifying these communication expectations, preventing misinterpretations and reinforcing a shared commitment to professionalism [145].

2. Active Listening as a Tool for Productive Dialogue

One of the most undervalued yet powerful tools for fostering effective communication in dissertation mentoring is active listening. Many conflicts and misunderstandings arise not from fundamental disagreements, but from miscommunication and perceived dismissiveness.

Active listening goes beyond simply hearing what is being said—it involves:

- **Engaging fully in the conversation:** Maintaining eye contact (for in-person discussions), nodding, or verbally acknowledging key points to show attentiveness.

- **Paraphrasing and summarizing points:** Confirming understanding by restating key ideas before responding (e.g., "So what I'm hearing is that you feel your methodology is being questioned, and you'd like more clarity on why.").

- **Asking clarifying questions:** Encouraging deeper discussion by prompting elaboration (e.g., "Can you explain how you arrived at that interpretation?").

- **Recognizing emotions behind statements:** Being attuned to whether frustration, anxiety, or discouragement is influencing the discussion, and responding with empathy [146].

For example, if a student appears defensive about committee feedback, rather than saying:

"You need to be open to feedback from your committee."

A chair practicing active listening might respond with:

"I understand that receiving feedback can sometimes feel overwhelming. Can you share which parts of the feedback are most challenging for you, so we can address them together?"

This reframes the conversation from criticism to collaboration, reducing defensiveness and paving the way for meaningful dialogue.

3. Managing and Resolving Conflicts Proactively

Dissertation research is an inherently high-stakes and complex process, and conflicts will arise—whether over research direction, theoretical framework selection, methodological choices, or committee dynamics.

A dissertation chair must anticipate these tensions and be prepared with structured conflict resolution strategies. When disagreements occur, it is essential to address them early and with a clear resolution plan to prevent prolonged disruptions.

Types of Dissertation Conflicts & How to Address Them

A. Student vs. Committee Conflicts

Students often struggle when they receive:

- **Conflicting feedback** from different committee members.

- **Excessive revisions** that make it difficult to maintain momentum.

- **Criticism that feels harsh or discouraging.**

Resolution Strategies:

1. **Clarify the Root of the Disagreement:** Encourage students to articulate exactly what aspect of the feedback they find confusing or challenging.

2. **Facilitate a Direct Discussion:** If feedback is conflicting, arrange a meeting where committee members can clarify their viewpoints and reach a consensus.

3. **Empower Students to Advocate for Their Research:** Encourage students to ask questions professionally, seek clarification, and engage in scholarly discourse rather than passively accepting feedback.

For example, instead of:

"Dr. X and Dr. Y have given me contradictory feedback. I don't know what to do."

A chair can coach the student to ask:

"Dr. X, you suggested refining my theoretical framework, while Dr. Y recommended keeping my original approach. Could we discuss how I can best align these perspectives in my study?"

This encourages students to own their research decisions while showing respectful engagement with their committee.

B. Committee vs. Committee Conflicts

At times, committee members may disagree with one another over theoretical interpretations, research methodology, or editorial recommendations. These disputes can create confusion for students and stall progress.

Resolution Strategies:

1. **Use the Chair as a Mediator:** The chair should step in to facilitate a structured conversation, ensuring that the discussion remains focused on academic rigor rather than personal biases.

2. **Identify Shared Goals:** Redirect the conversation toward the overarching goal of strengthening the dissertation, rather than debating who is "right."

3. **Encourage Compromise:** When necessary, chairs should work toward a middle-ground approach that satisfies committee concerns without compromising the integrity of the student's work.

If tensions remain unresolved, the chair may need to hold private discussions with committee members to prevent disputes from negatively affecting the student's experience.

C. Chair vs. Student Conflicts

Sometimes, a student may disagree with their chair's guidance or feel unsupported in their research process.

Resolution Strategies:

1. **Acknowledge the Student's Concerns:** Even if a chair disagrees, validating the student's perspective can help de-escalate tension.

2. **Encourage a Collaborative Approach:** Rather than a rigid hierarchy, frame the conversation as a mutual effort to strengthen the research.

3. **Provide Transparent Rationale:** If a chair insists on a certain change, they should explain the reasoning behind their decision in clear academic terms rather than enforcing authority without context.

For example, instead of:

"You need to change your methodology because I said so."

A chair might say:

"I understand why you want to use this approach, but based on best practices in your field, this method has limitations that could affect the validity of your findings. Would you be open to exploring an alternative?"

This approach encourages dialogue without dismissing the student's intellectual agency.

4. Preventing Future Conflicts Through Proactive Leadership

While conflict resolution is important, preventing unnecessary conflicts before they arise is even more critical. Chairs can reduce the likelihood of misunderstandings by:

- **Setting clear expectations upfront** (through Dissertation Agreements and structured timelines).

- **Facilitating regular check-ins** to address concerns before they escalate.

- **Encouraging transparency in committee decisions** to prevent students from receiving conflicting guidance.

- **Modeling professionalism and scholarly engagement** in all interactions.

By creating a structured, respectful, and solution-focused academic environment, dissertation chairs can transform potential conflicts into opportunities for deeper scholarly engagement and intellectual growth.

Conclusion

Fostering productive dialogue and resolving conflicts in dissertation mentorship is essential for student success. By setting clear communication norms, employing active listening techniques, mediating disputes professionally, and preventing conflicts through proactive leadership, dissertation chairs can create a collaborative, structured, and academically rigorous environment where students thrive.

A well-handled discussion can instill confidence, build resilience, and keep research momentum moving forward, ultimately ensuring that students graduate not only as scholars but as empowered, independent researchers.

Setting Clear Expectations for Student and Committee Collaboration

A well-structured dissertation process relies on clear expectations and transparent communication between students, chairs, and committee members. Dissertation research is inherently complex, requiring a structured yet flexible approach to ensure that both academic rigor and student progress are maintained. Without defined expectations, students may struggle with inconsistent feedback, unclear timelines, or avoidable miscommunications that can delay their progress. Similarly, committee members benefit from knowing their roles, responsibilities, and the expectations for their engagement, ensuring a smooth and effective dissertation review process.

From the outset, dissertation chairs should establish well-defined roles, responsibilities, and communication norms for all involved. A structured dissertation roadmap—outlining key milestones, submission deadlines, meeting schedules, and feedback turnaround times—provides all stakeholders with a shared understanding of how the process will unfold. This clarity helps prevent unnecessary delays, confusion, and frustration, enabling students to stay on track while receiving the guidance they need.

This section explores best practices for setting clear expectations for student and committee collaboration, emphasizing the importance of formal agreements, structured communication strategies, proactive engagement with feedback, and regular progress check-ins. By implementing these strategies, dissertation chairs and committees can create a productive academic environment that fosters student success.

1. Establishing a Dissertation Agreement: The Power of Formal Expectations

One of the most effective ways to ensure clarity and accountability is through the development of a Dissertation Agreement or Memorandum of Understanding (MOU). This document serves as a contractual guide that outlines the responsibilities of all parties, ensuring that expectations are not only verbalized but also documented for reference throughout the dissertation process.

Key Elements of a Dissertation Agreement

A well-structured Dissertation Agreement should cover:

- **Roles and Responsibilities:**
  - The dissertation chair's role in guiding the student through research design, methodology, and academic writing.
  - The committee members' role in providing expertise, offering feedback, and approving key dissertation milestones.
  - The student's responsibilities in meeting deadlines, incorporating feedback, and proactively managing their dissertation process.

- **Communication Expectations:**
  - Preferred methods of communication (email, virtual meetings, in-person consultations).
  - Response time expectations for emails, meeting requests, and document reviews.
  - Guidelines for professional and respectful communication among all parties.

- **Feedback Turnaround Times:**
  - Timeframes for reviewing dissertation chapters (e.g., committee members should provide feedback within 2-3 weeks of receiving a draft).
  - Clear expectations for how feedback should be structured (e.g., providing constructive, specific guidance rather than vague comments).

- **Process for Addressing Challenges:**
  - A structured approach for handling disagreements over methodology, data analysis, or theoretical frameworks.
  - Steps for mediation if conflicts arise between the student and committee members.
  - A procedure for requesting an advisor or committee member change if necessary.

Benefits of a Formal Agreement

A Dissertation Agreement minimizes ambiguity and promotes accountability by ensuring that all stakeholders operate with a shared understanding of expectations [147]. Additionally, formalizing these guidelines:

- Prevents last-minute surprises related to deadlines and feedback expectations.

- Reduces student anxiety by providing clear guidelines for engagement.

- Encourages consistency among committee members, preventing conflicting feedback.

- Establishes a reference point for resolving disputes or misunderstandings.

Dissertation chairs should introduce this agreement early in the dissertation process—ideally at the first committee meeting—to ensure alignment from the beginning.

2. Navigating the Committee Dynamic: Preparing Students for Constructive Engagement

Beyond setting broad expectations, dissertation chairs must help students develop the skills necessary to engage effectively with their committee. Many doctoral candidates enter the dissertation phase with limited experience in managing faculty feedback, understanding academic critique, or reconciling differing perspectives from multiple advisors.

Chairs should actively prepare students to navigate committee interactions, particularly in terms of receiving and incorporating feedback, structuring their questions effectively, and maintaining professional communication.

Teaching Students to Seek and Apply Feedback Proactively

Dissertation research is an iterative process—students must expect and embrace multiple rounds of revisions [148]. Chairs should encourage students to:

- **Be proactive in clarifying feedback** rather than assuming that every critique is a rejection of their work.

- **Avoid waiting until a full chapter is written** before seeking input—early-stage feedback helps prevent major rewrites later.

- **Recognize that feedback is part of the scholarly dialogue** and not a personal critique of their abilities.

For example, if a student receives conflicting feedback from two committee members, the chair should guide them in how to reconcile these differences:

- **Ask clarifying questions**: "Can you elaborate on how this suggested revision aligns with my research objectives?"

- **Synthesize differing viewpoints**: Identify common themes in feedback and discuss solutions with the chair.

- **Prioritize actionable revisions**: Determine which changes will have the greatest impact on the dissertation's clarity and scholarly contribution.

Framing Questions to Maximize Clarity and Effectiveness

Dissertation chairs should also teach students how to frame their questions in a way that elicits actionable responses. Vague, open-ended inquiries often result in generic or conflicting advice, whereas targeted questions help committee members provide meaningful input.

For example, instead of: *"What do you think of my literature review?"*

Encourage students to ask: *"Does my literature review sufficiently establish the theoretical gap in my research? Are there specific sources or frameworks I should explore further?"*

By framing questions with specificity, students increase the likelihood of receiving precise, constructive feedback that moves their dissertation forward.

3. Regular Check-Ins: Ensuring Ongoing Alignment and Progress

Setting expectations is not a one-time event; it requires ongoing reinforcement through structured check-ins. Regular touchpoints between chairs, students, and committee members help maintain alignment, identify potential issues early, and keep the dissertation process moving forward smoothly.

Types of Dissertation Check-Ins

1. **Formal Committee Meetings (Every 3-6 Months)**

   o   Review major dissertation milestones.

   o   Discuss overall progress and anticipated challenges.

   o   Ensure committee feedback is aligned and consistent [149].

2. **One-on-One Chair Meetings (Monthly or Biweekly)**

   o   Provide targeted guidance on research, writing, and time management.

   o   Address any emerging concerns before they escalate [149].

3. **Email or Informal Check-Ins (As Needed)**

   o   Quick updates to ensure the student remains on track.

   o   Opportunity for students to ask clarifying questions between formal meetings [149].

Adjusting Expectations When Necessary

Even with the best planning, unexpected challenges arise—students may face personal hardships, research obstacles, or changes in their dissertation direction. Chairs should be flexible in recalibrating timelines and expectations, when necessary, provided that adjustments maintain academic rigor.

For instance:

- If a student encounters unexpected data collection delays, the chair can help them adjust their research schedule while keeping progress steady.

- If a committee member is consistently unresponsive, the chair should intervene to ensure the student receives timely feedback [150].

These regular check-ins create an environment where students feel supported while ensuring that accountability remains a priority.

4. Building a Collaborative and Trust-Based Culture

At its core, setting clear expectations is about fostering a culture of mutual respect, collaboration, and academic excellence. Chairs should model the communication strategies they expect from students and committee members—demonstrating professionalism, responsiveness, and a commitment to student success.

Key elements of a collaborative dissertation culture include:

- **Consistency in communication:** When expectations are consistently reinforced, students and committees function more effectively.

- **Transparency in decision-making:** When students understand why certain decisions are made, they are more likely to trust and engage with the process.

- **Encouraging student agency:** While dissertation chairs provide guidance, students must take ownership of their research, communication, and progress.

By prioritizing these values, dissertation chairs reduce confusion, prevent misunderstandings, and create an academic environment where students and faculty work together productively.

Conclusion

Establishing clear expectations for student and committee collaboration is essential for a successful, structured, and effective dissertation process. Through formal Dissertation Agreements, proactive student guidance, regular check-ins, and a culture of trust and collaboration, dissertation chairs can ensure that students receive the mentorship, feedback, and academic support needed to navigate their doctoral journey with confidence.

When expectations are well-defined and consistently reinforced, students thrive, committee members remain engaged, and the dissertation process becomes a pathway to scholarly success rather than a source of confusion and frustration.

Managing Difficult Conversations and Handling Student Concerns

In the rigorous landscape of doctoral education, dissertation chairs and committees inevitably encounter challenging conversations with students. These discussions may stem from concerns about a student's lack of progress, methodological missteps, or conflicts over academic integrity. At times, students may struggle with feedback, exhibit defensive behaviors, or face personal and professional difficulties that impact their research trajectory. How these conversations are handled can make the difference between a student feeling supported and motivated or becoming disengaged and discouraged.

Difficult conversations are not merely administrative necessities; they are pivotal moments in a doctoral candidate's academic journey. A well-handled discussion can instill confidence, promote self-awareness, and guide students toward solutions that empower them to persevere. Conversely, a poorly managed conversation can create tension, erode trust, and even contribute to student attrition. Thus, dissertation chairs must approach these conversations with a combination of diplomacy, empathy, and a firm commitment to academic rigor.

This section explores key strategies for navigating difficult conversations in ways that encourage student growth while maintaining professional standards. By focusing on solution-oriented dialogue, active empathy, and structured intervention strategies, dissertation chairs and committees can cultivate an environment that fosters resilience, accountability, and scholarly excellence.

1. Adopting a Solution-Oriented Approach

A primary goal of managing difficult conversations is to shift the focus from problems to solutions. Instead of dwelling on what a student is doing wrong, dissertation chairs should redirect the discussion toward constructive steps for improvement. This approach transforms potentially adversarial conversations into opportunities for growth.

Reframing the Conversation

Rather than saying:
"You have missed multiple deadlines, and this is unacceptable."

A solution-oriented chair might say:
"I noticed that you've struggled with deadlines recently. Let's talk about what challenges you're facing and how we can adjust your timeline to set you up for success."

This subtle shift in language removes blame and opens a collaborative space where the student can take ownership of their progress while feeling supported.

Providing Clear Action Steps

Instead of simply stating what needs improvement, chairs should guide students through specific, realistic, and measurable actions. If a student is behind on writing, rather than demanding immediate progress, a chair might suggest:

- **Breaking tasks into smaller milestones** (e.g., completing one section per week).

- **Using accountability tools** (e.g., scheduled check-ins or progress logs).

- **Exploring time management techniques** (e.g., setting research goals with structured deadlines).

- **Seeking external support** (e.g., writing centers, peer review groups).

By giving students a roadmap forward, chairs can empower them to take proactive steps instead of feeling overwhelmed by academic expectations.

2. Practicing Active Empathy in Student Interactions

Doctoral students navigate a complex web of challenges—intellectual, emotional, financial, and professional. Many juggle full-time jobs, family obligations, and research responsibilities while dealing with imposter syndrome, perfectionism, or self-doubt. Some students may hesitate to share their struggles for fear of appearing weak, while others may become defensive when receiving critical feedback.

A dissertation chair's ability to listen with empathy can significantly impact a student's confidence and engagement. Active empathy involves more than offering kind words—it requires genuinely seeking to understand the student's perspective, validating their experiences, and responding in a way that balances academic expectations with human-centered support.

Techniques for Active Empathy

- **Non-Judgmental Listening:** Let the student express their concerns fully before responding. Avoid interrupting or immediately offering solutions.

- **Reflective Statements:** Summarize what the student has shared to confirm understanding (e.g., *"It sounds like balancing work and research has been particularly difficult for you."*).

- **Acknowledging Struggles:** Show that you recognize the student's challenges without lowering academic expectations (e.g., *"I know this process can feel overwhelming, and I appreciate your commitment to moving forward."*).

- **Offering Perspective:** Help students reframe setbacks as learning opportunities (e.g., *"Every researcher faces obstacles. The key is developing strategies to overcome them, and I'm here to help you with that."*).

By demonstrating genuine care, chairs can encourage students to be more open about their difficulties, allowing for earlier intervention and more effective support.

3. Navigating Defensiveness and Disengagement

At times, students may react to feedback with defensiveness, avoidance, or outright disengagement. Some may become argumentative, resisting guidance or justifying shortcomings. Others may retreat, failing to respond to emails or skipping meetings. These behaviors often stem from anxiety, fear of failure, or feeling overwhelmed.

Dissertation chairs must address these behaviors early before they escalate into prolonged stagnation or complete disengagement. The key is to balance patience with firmness—creating an environment where students feel safe to express concerns while maintaining clear academic expectations.

Dealing with Defensiveness

A defensive student may respond to constructive feedback with excuses, counterarguments, or frustration. When faced with this, chairs should:

- **Stay calm and avoid escalating the conflict.** Keep responses professional and non-confrontational.

- **Acknowledge the student's feelings.** ("I understand that this feedback may be difficult to hear, but my goal is to help strengthen your work.")

- **Redirect the focus to solutions.** Encourage students to view feedback as a tool for growth rather than criticism.

For example, instead of debating whether a literature review is "good enough," a chair might say:
"I see where you're coming from, and I appreciate the effort you've put in. Let's work together to refine this section so it aligns with scholarly expectations."

This shifts the conversation from a defensive stance to a collaborative effort.

Re-Engaging a Disengaged Student

Some students, rather than pushing back, may begin avoiding communication altogether. In these cases:

- **Reach out with genuine concern.** A simple email like *"I haven't heard from you in a while—how are things going?"* can prompt a response.

- **Offer flexible but firm accountability.** If personal struggles are causing disengagement, chairs can propose adjusted but structured milestones to help the student regain momentum.

- **Encourage the use of institutional resources.** Writing centers, counseling services, and faculty mentors can provide additional support when students feel isolated.

If a student remains unresponsive after multiple outreach attempts, chairs may need to escalate concerns to program administrators to determine the best course of action [151].

4. Reinforcing a Growth Mindset

At its core, managing difficult conversations is about reinforcing a growth mindset—the belief that challenges, setbacks, and constructive criticism are opportunities for learning rather than indicators of failure. Dissertation chairs play a critical role in helping students reframe difficulties in ways that build resilience and scholarly independence.

Key strategies for reinforcing a growth mindset include:

- **Normalizing struggle**: Remind students that all doctoral candidates face challenges, and struggling is part of the learning process.

- **Emphasizing progress over perfection**: Help students focus on steady improvements rather than expecting flawless drafts.

- **Encouraging intellectual curiosity**: Frame research setbacks as opportunities to refine thinking rather than as failures.

For example, instead of saying:
"You need to completely rethink your research design because it's flawed."

A chair might say:
"Your research design has some challenges, but refining it will strengthen your study. Let's explore alternative approaches that could yield stronger results."

By embedding positivity, accountability, and problem-solving into difficult conversations, dissertation chairs help students develop the confidence and skills needed to succeed—not just in their doctoral program, but in their future academic and professional careers.

Conclusion

Managing difficult conversations is an integral part of dissertation mentorship. By adopting a solution-oriented approach, practicing active empathy, addressing defensiveness and disengagement with patience, and reinforcing a growth mindset, dissertation chairs and committees can create an academic environment that nurtures both intellectual and personal development. These strategies ensure that challenges become learning experiences, fostering a collaborative, empowering, and rigorous doctoral journey for every student.

Accountability Without Escalation: Preparing for a Performance Conversation

Addressing student performance concerns is one of the most consequential responsibilities of a dissertation chair. When progress stalls, professionalism declines, deadlines are missed, or expectations are not met, the temptation is to react quickly—often in frustration, often without preparation.

Unstructured confrontation rarely produces growth. Silence rarely produces correction. Effective leadership requires something else: preparation.

A performance conversation at the doctoral level is not a reprimand. It is a structured intervention designed to restore clarity, accountability, and forward momentum. The goal is not to assert authority. The goal is to realign standards and expectations while preserving professional dignity.

When chairs fail to prepare, conversations become:

- Vague
- Emotionally charged
- Defensively received

- Poorly documented
- Difficult to escalate appropriately

When chairs prepare intentionally, conversations become:

- Evidence-based
- Clear
- Fair
- Action-oriented
- Protective of both student and institution

Before initiating a difficult conversation, pause. Calibrate. Ensure you are addressing behavior—not projecting frustration. Ensure expectations are documented—not implied. Ensure support is offered—not withheld.

Use the following checklist to prepare yourself before addressing student performance concerns.

Performance Intervention Preparation Checklist

Before Addressing Student Performance Issues:

☐ I have documented specific examples of the concern (dates, behaviors, missed milestones, communication patterns).

☐ I have identified the measurable impact or consequence of the issue (timeline delays, research quality risks, committee concerns, compliance risks).

☐ I have clarified the expected standard, behavior, or performance requirement.

☐ I have prepared appropriate support resources (writing center, research methods support, time management tools, counseling referral pathways, etc.).

☐ I have scheduled private, uninterrupted meeting time.

☐ I am prepared to listen without defensiveness or interruption.

☐ I have developed a clear action plan with specific benchmarks and deadlines.

☐ I understand the institutional escalation path if progress does not improve (program director, formal warning, committee review, etc.).

Chapter 15 - Time Management for Dissertation Chairs

Figure 15. [222].

Time management is a crucial skill for dissertation chairs, who must balance multiple responsibilities while effectively guiding doctoral candidates through their research journey. Managing dissertation supervision requires careful planning, prioritization, and structured support to ensure that both students and faculty members can navigate the complex dissertation process without unnecessary delays or burnout [152]. Without proper time management strategies, dissertation chairs may struggle to provide timely feedback, students may experience stagnation, and the overall dissertation process may become inefficient and frustrating [153].

Doctoral research is a long-term commitment that involves multiple stages, including topic selection, literature review, data collection, analysis, and writing. Throughout this process, dissertation chairs serve as key mentors, offering direction, reviewing drafts, and ensuring that students adhere to institutional timelines. Given that many faculty members oversee multiple doctoral candidates while also managing teaching, research, and administrative duties, adopting effective time management practices is essential for maintaining productivity and student success [154].

The primary components of time management in dissertation supervision include:

- **Managing Multiple Students Effectively** – Dissertation chairs often mentor several students at different stages of research. Implementing structured schedules, prioritizing tasks, and leveraging digital tools can help streamline supervision and maintain progress for all students.

- **Setting Boundaries While Maintaining Accessibility** – While responsiveness is critical, chairs must establish clear boundaries to prevent burnout and maintain a sustainable workload. Setting defined office hours, turnaround times for feedback, and structured meeting agendas ensures efficiency without compromising support.

- **Handling Delays, Extensions, and Student Disengagement** – Research challenges, personal circumstances, and motivation issues can lead to student delays. Dissertation chairs must develop proactive strategies to address stagnation, provide accountability structures, and help students stay on track.

Effective time management benefits both dissertation chairs and students. When faculty members allocate their time efficiently, they can provide high-quality mentorship without becoming overwhelmed by competing responsibilities [155]. Additionally, well-structured timelines and milestone tracking foster student motivation, ensuring that doctoral candidates maintain steady progress toward dissertation completion [156].

This chapter provides a comprehensive guide to time management strategies tailored specifically for dissertation chairs. It offers insights into best practices for balancing multiple students, setting boundaries while remaining accessible, and addressing common delays in the dissertation process. By implementing these strategies, dissertation chairs can create a structured and productive mentorship environment that supports both faculty well-being and student success.

Managing Multiple Students Effectively

Dissertation chairs are often responsible for overseeing multiple doctoral candidates simultaneously, each at different stages of their research [157]. Effective time management is essential to providing equitable support while maintaining high academic standards [158].

Key strategies for managing multiple students efficiently include:

- **Establishing Clear Schedules and Milestones:** Chairs should create structured timelines for each student, outlining key dissertation phases, deadlines, and expectations. Digital project management tools like Trello, Asana, or shared Google Sheets can help track progress and ensure accountability.

- **Prioritizing Based on Student Needs:** Not all students require the same level of attention at all times. Some may be in data collection phases, while others are refining their literature reviews. Chairs should assess where intervention is most needed and allocate time accordingly.

- **Conducting Regular Check-ins:** Scheduling biweekly or monthly one-on-one meetings helps keep students on track and minimizes last-minute crises. These meetings should focus on research progress, challenges, and actionable next steps.

- **Using Group Meetings Strategically:** Organizing periodic group discussions allows students to share experiences, learn from one another, and reduce the burden of repeated individual sessions.

- **Encouraging Self-Sufficiency:** While guidance is crucial, chairs should also encourage students to develop problem-solving skills, seek peer feedback, and utilize institutional resources before escalating issues.

By implementing these time management strategies, dissertation chairs can ensure that each student receives the attention and guidance necessary while maintaining a sustainable workload.

Setting Boundaries While Maintaining Accessibility

A dissertation chair's role requires balancing responsiveness with personal time management. Being accessible to students is critical, but without setting firm boundaries, chairs risk burnout and inefficiency.

Strategies for setting professional yet supportive boundaries include:

- **Defining Office Hours and Availability:** Clearly communicating specific times when students can expect responses to emails or schedule meetings helps manage expectations and prevents constant interruptions.

- **Utilizing Asynchronous Communication Tools:** Encouraging students to send structured questions via email or shared documents allows chairs to provide feedback at convenient times rather than responding to ad hoc inquiries.

- **Implementing Structured Meeting Agendas:** Ensuring that every meeting has a defined agenda prevents unnecessary discussions and maximizes productivity.

- **Encouraging Proactive Planning:** Students should be guided to schedule meetings in advance and prepare discussion points rather than expecting on-demand availability.

- **Establishing Turnaround Times for Feedback:** Chairs should communicate realistic response times for reviewing drafts, preventing students from expecting immediate reviews and allowing for balanced time allocation.

By setting firm yet flexible boundaries, dissertation chairs can provide quality mentorship while ensuring that their own workload remains manageable and sustainable.

Handling Delays, Extensions, and Student Disengagement

Despite best efforts, delays in dissertation progress are common due to various academic, personal, and logistical challenges [159]. Dissertation chairs must be equipped with strategies to address setbacks while keeping students motivated and accountable.

Managing Delays and Extensions

- **Identifying the Root Cause:** Chairs should determine whether delays stem from methodological roadblocks, personal issues, or lack of motivation. Understanding the source helps tailor interventions effectively.

- **Developing a Revised Timeline:** When delays occur, chairs should help students create an updated, realistic work plan with smaller, manageable milestones to regain momentum.

- **Institutional Compliance:** Chairs must ensure that any extensions comply with university policies and necessary approvals are obtained in a timely manner.

Addressing Student Disengagement

- **Recognizing Early Warning Signs:** Reduced communication, missed deadlines, and minimal progress updates can indicate disengagement. Chairs should be proactive in reaching out before the situation escalates.

- **Providing Encouragement and Motivation:** Some students lose confidence in their research abilities. Regular affirmations, constructive feedback, and reminding them of their academic goals can reignite commitment.

- **Offering Alternative Support Mechanisms:** Some students may benefit from writing coaches, peer accountability groups, or mental health resources to help them navigate challenges.

- **Establishing Clear Expectations:** If disengagement persists, chairs should document communications, set firm deadlines, and, when necessary, escalate the matter to academic advisors or department heads.

By effectively managing delays, setting realistic expectations, and proactively addressing disengagement, dissertation chairs can help students navigate obstacles while ensuring that progress toward completion remains a priority.

Conclusion

Time management for dissertation chairs is an essential skill that ensures students receive effective mentorship while faculty members maintain balance in their responsibilities. By managing multiple students strategically, setting boundaries to preserve accessibility, and addressing delays and disengagement with proactive solutions, dissertation chairs can foster a productive and supportive academic environment. Implementing these best practices not only benefits students but also enhances the overall efficiency and effectiveness of dissertation supervision.

Section 4: Institutional Engagement and Continuous Improvement

Figure S4. [222].

There is a moment in every doctoral journey—often unspoken—when the question quietly shifts. It is no longer *How do I guide this student?* It becomes *What kind of system am I helping sustain?*

Up to this point, *The Master Key* has focused on the individual acts of leadership that define effective dissertation supervision: ethical mentorship, rigorous feedback, argumentation, communication, and time stewardship. These are the craft skills of the dissertation chair. They matter. They change lives.

But craft alone is not enough. Part IV marks a deliberate transition—from individual excellence to institutional responsibility. From mentoring students to shaping the ecosystem in which mentorship occurs. From surviving within flawed systems to having the courage to improve them.

Together, these chapters assert a simple but disruptive truth:

- Doctoral education does not improve by accident.
- It improves when faculty choose to lead—beyond their inboxes, beyond tradition, and beyond their own dissertations.

Part IV is not about adding more work to already full academic lives. It is about reclaiming *agency*. About recognizing that chairs are not merely participants in the system—they are stewards of it.

This final section invites you to step fully into that role. Not as a gatekeeper. Not as a survivor of academic dysfunction. But as a leader willing to align mentorship, policy, and purpose.

The Master Key does not end with process. It ends with responsibility.

Chapter 16 - Faculty Development and Professional Growth

The role of a dissertation chair extends far beyond guiding students through the research process; it encompasses continuous learning, professional growth, and institutional engagement. Faculty development is essential for dissertation chairs to stay updated on best practices in research mentorship, emerging methodologies, and evolving academic standards [160]. As higher education continues to transform, faculty members must actively seek opportunities for professional growth to enhance their effectiveness as mentors and leaders in doctoral education.

Figure 16. [222].

Dissertation chairs play a pivotal role in shaping the academic and professional trajectories of doctoral candidates [161]. Their responsibilities include mentoring students, ensuring research integrity, navigating institutional policies, and fostering an environment conducive to scholarly excellence [162]. However, to fulfill these responsibilities effectively, dissertation chairs must engage in ongoing professional development that sharpens their skills, deepens their expertise, and enables them to navigate the complexities of dissertation supervision with confidence and efficiency.

The key aspects of faculty development for dissertation chairs include:

- **Engaging in Ongoing Dissertation Chair Training** – Institutions should offer regular training programs to help dissertation chairs stay informed about best practices in supervision, research methodologies, and student engagement strategies [163].

- **Learning from Successful Dissertation Chair Experiences** – Examining case studies, participating in faculty mentoring programs, and sharing insights with experienced dissertation chairs can provide valuable perspectives on effective dissertation supervision.

- **Staying Current with Research Trends and Emerging Methodologies** – As academic disciplines evolve, dissertation chairs must remain knowledgeable about new research methodologies, technological advancements, and interdisciplinary approaches that may impact doctoral research [164].

Faculty development is not only beneficial for dissertation chairs but also contributes to the overall strength of doctoral programs. When chairs receive proper training and professional support, they are better equipped to mentor students effectively, address common research challenges, and uphold academic integrity. Moreover, institutions that invest in faculty development create a culture of continuous improvement, enhancing the quality of doctoral education and research output.

This chapter explores the essential components of faculty development and professional growth for dissertation chairs. It provides strategies for engaging in training programs, learning from experienced mentors, and staying current with research trends. By prioritizing faculty development, dissertation chairs can refine their mentorship skills, support doctoral candidates more effectively, and contribute to a thriving academic community.

Engaging in Ongoing Dissertation Chair Training

The role of a dissertation chair extends far beyond administrative oversight; it requires a deep commitment to mentorship, scholarship, and academic leadership. To ensure that dissertation chairs are equipped to guide doctoral candidates effectively, ongoing professional development is essential.

Importance of Continuous Training

Academic institutions must prioritize structured training programs for dissertation chairs, recognizing that the landscape of doctoral education is continuously evolving [165]. Effective training ensures that chairs:

- **Remain proficient in emerging research methodologies** that shape dissertation structures and execution.

- **Enhance their mentorship skills** to accommodate diverse student needs, learning styles, and research interests.

- **Develop expertise in conflict resolution and academic coaching** to help students navigate challenges and setbacks.

- **Understand institutional policies and accreditation standards** that impact dissertation expectations and compliance [166].

Methods for Continuous Learning

1. **Institutional Workshops & Seminars** – Universities should offer periodic training sessions covering best practices in dissertation supervision, student motivation strategies, and ethical research considerations [167].

2. **Peer Learning & Faculty Discussion Groups** – Facilitating knowledge-sharing sessions where experienced dissertation chairs discuss challenges and solutions fosters an environment of collective growth [168].

3. **Online Courses & Certifications** – Many institutions and research organizations offer specialized online programs on dissertation mentorship, qualitative and quantitative methodologies, and emerging trends in higher education [169].

4. **Annual Evaluations & Feedback Mechanisms** – Regular assessments and structured feedback from students and colleagues help chairs refine their approach to dissertation supervision [170].

By actively engaging in training opportunities, dissertation chairs not only improve their effectiveness but also contribute to an institutional culture of excellence in doctoral education.

Learning from Successful Dissertation Chair Experiences

While formal training is invaluable, experiential learning remains one of the most powerful tools for faculty development. By analyzing and reflecting on the strategies of successful dissertation chairs, faculty members can cultivate best practices that lead to more effective student guidance [171].

Case Studies and Best Practices

1. **Encouraging Early Research Development** – Highly effective chairs emphasize the importance of developing research ideas early in the doctoral program, guiding students through literature reviews and theoretical framing well before formal dissertation proposals [172].

2. **Establishing a Structured Mentorship Approach** – Successful chairs implement structured mentoring frameworks, including scheduled meetings, milestone tracking, and clear communication protocols 173].

3. **Navigating Challenges with Diplomacy and Support** – Faculty members who excel in dissertation leadership foster resilience in their students, offering solutions-oriented feedback rather than punitive critiques [174].

4. **Building Strong Committee Collaboration** – Effective chairs maintain positive relationships with dissertation committee members, ensuring alignment in feedback and decision-making processes.

5. **Leveraging Technology for Supervision** – Innovative dissertation chairs use project management tools, collaborative writing platforms, and virtual meetings to maintain accessibility and efficiency in the dissertation process [175].

Institutionalizing Shared Knowledge

- **Faculty Mentorship Programs** – Senior dissertation chairs should mentor new faculty, offering guidance on managing multiple students, fostering intellectual independence, and addressing common dissertation pitfalls [176].

- **Case Study Analysis Sessions** – Institutions should encourage the documentation and discussion of successful dissertation guidance cases to establish best-practice models [177].

- **Cross-Disciplinary Learning** – Chairs can benefit from engaging with faculty across disciplines to explore diverse approaches to dissertation supervision and academic mentorship [178].

By embracing experiential learning and adopting proven strategies, dissertation chairs enhance their effectiveness and contribute to the overall success of doctoral candidates.

Staying Current with Research Trends and Emerging Methodologies

As academic disciplines evolve, dissertation chairs must stay abreast of emerging research trends and methodologies to provide relevant and informed guidance. The rapid advancement of technology, data analytics, and interdisciplinary research necessitates a proactive approach to scholarly engagement [179].

Key Areas for Continuous Learning

1. **Emerging Methodological Frameworks** – Chairs should explore the latest developments in qualitative, quantitative, and mixed-methods research approaches to ensure that students are utilizing the most appropriate and robust methodologies [180].

2. **Interdisciplinary and Applied Research Trends** – Faculty must encourage students to explore interdisciplinary research, particularly in fields where cross-disciplinary integration enhances the depth and applicability of doctoral studies [181].

3. **Technological Innovations in Research** – The use of artificial intelligence, big data analytics, and digital ethnography is reshaping research methodologies. Chairs should familiarize themselves with these tools to support students incorporating them into their dissertations [182].

4. **Ethical Considerations in Modern Research** – As new research methods emerge, ethical concerns evolve. Dissertation chairs must stay informed about institutional review board (IRB) policies, data privacy regulations, and responsible research practices [183].

Strategies for Staying Informed

- **Regularly Attending Academic Conferences** – Engaging in research symposia and academic conferences keeps faculty updated on cutting-edge developments in their respective fields [184].

- **Subscribing to Leading Journals and Publications** – Staying current with top-tier academic journals helps chairs recommend relevant literature to students and incorporate new findings into dissertation discussions [185].

- **Participating in Research Collaborations** – Engaging in joint research projects allows faculty to experience emerging methodologies firsthand and apply them in dissertation mentorship.

- **Engaging in Professional Networks** – Membership in academic organizations and research consortiums fosters continuous learning and access to expert discussions [186].

By staying current with research trends and methodologies, dissertation chairs empower students to produce innovative, high-impact research that aligns with contemporary academic and professional expectations [187].

Staying Current with Emerging Research Technologies

AI in Doctoral Education: Leading Through Disruption

The landscape of doctoral education is evolving—and not in theory, but in real time. Across classrooms, proposal meetings, and defense rehearsals, a new kind of cognitive presence is quietly shaping the way students read, write, and reason: **generative AI [188]**.

While some faculty still regard these tools as a passing trend or fringe experiment, others are watching them transform scholarly habits at a foundational level. Whether through literature synthesis engines like *Elicit* or *Scite*, AI-assisted citation tools like *Scribbr*, or large language models such as *ChatGPT*, students are engaging in doctoral work in ways that didn't exist even five years ago [189].

The question is not whether AI will impact our mentorship practices. The question is whether we, as faculty, are prepared to respond ethically, pedagogically, and with vision.

A New Kind of Dissertation Workflow

To truly understand this shift, we must examine how generative AI is being used—not just as a novelty, but as a functional partner in the dissertation process. The impact is not isolated; it spans the entire lifecycle of doctoral work.

Literature Review Synthesis

Students today can upload PDFs into a tool like *Elicit*, which then extracts key findings, compares methodologies, and clusters thematic elements. Tools like *Scite* rank articles based on credibility and citation networks. This accelerates the early stages of review but also flattens nuance. Contradictory findings, fringe perspectives, and theoretical inconsistencies can be easily missed [190].

Faculty challenge: How do we train students to go beyond pattern recognition and engage in deep, dialectical analysis?

APA Formatting and Citation Management

Gone are the days of combing through citation manuals. AI tools like *Scribbr* and *EndNote* now auto-format references, check DOIs, and even identify missing in-text citations. While this enhances technical polish, it can also erode the student's understanding of why citations matter [191].

Faculty challenge: Are students developing fluency in source attribution—or simply offloading it?

Concept Mapping and Research Design

With a single prompt, tools like *ChatGPT* can generate sample research questions, build hypothetical conceptual frameworks, and even suggest methodological pairings. This is helpful for brainstorming but dangerous when accepted uncritically. Students risk mistaking linguistic plausibility for methodological rigor [192].

Faculty challenge: Are students being trained to interrogate logic and defend their frameworks—or just to accept whatever sounds scholarly?

Risk and Responsibility in the Age of Augmented Scholarship

It would be a mistake to frame AI in doctoral education as either a salvation or a scourge. It is neither. It is, instead, a mirror—a reflection of how modern scholars think, cope, and create. And like any mirror, it demands interpretation.

We cannot afford to ignore this shift.

Prohibition will not stop usage. It will only ensure that usage happens in the shadows— unquestioned, unformed, and unethically applied [194].
Our role as faculty must evolve. We must step forward not just as reviewers of written work, but as stewards of intellectual integrity in a transformed landscape.

That means:

- Initiating open conversations about AI early in the dissertation process.
- Offering frameworks for ethical and appropriate usage.
- Redefining authorship not just as output, but as cognitive ownership.
- Evaluating students not solely on how polished their writing is, but on how deeply they understand, defend, and synthesize their work.

Practical Guidance: When AI Helps—and When It Harms

Below is a guide for faculty and chairs seeking clarity on AI's role in the dissertation process. Use this as a checkpoint during meetings, proposal reviews, or committee discussions.

AI Use Case	Tool Type	Faculty Stance	Caution Flags
Literature Synthesis	Elicit, Scite, ChatGPT	Use to spot themes early	Can oversimplify nuance, omit contradictory findings
APA Formatting and Citations	Scribbr, EndNote	Streamline mechanics	AI may hallucinate sources or misuse secondary citations
Question Brainstorming	ChatGPT, Perplexity	Use for early ideation	Student may adopt weak or vague questions without refinement

AI Use Case	Tool Type	Faculty Stance	Caution Flags
Concept Mapping	Lucidchart w/ AI, ChatGPT	Visual aid for thinking	Logical connections may lack empirical grounding
Writing Enhancement	GrammarlyGO, Hemingway Editor	Improve tone and flow	May suppress unique voice or introduce generic phrasing
Code/Syntax Support	ChatGPT, GitHub Copilot	Good for debugging or guidance	Must validate output manually—especially for statistical analysis or logic

Conclusion

Faculty development is not a box to be checked—it is an ongoing act of intellectual renewal. As the landscape of doctoral education continues to evolve, so too must we evolve—not only in what we teach, but in *how* we think, engage, and lead.

This chapter has emphasized staying current is not merely about consuming new research or attending occasional conferences. It is about embracing a mindset of adaptive scholarship, where change is not feared but examined, and where emerging methodologies—especially those shaped by AI—are met with discernment rather than dismissal.

The future of doctoral mentorship will not be shaped by those who cling to legacy models, nor by those who outsource their wisdom to machines. It will be shaped by those who:

- Remain grounded in core academic values while adapting to new tools and paradigms.
- Engage students as co-researchers and evolving professionals, not passive recipients of instruction.
- Reframe AI, digital tools, and data-driven methodologies not as threats, but as invitations to reimagine scholarly practice with ethical clarity and creative courage.

To be a chair in this era is to become a translator of complexity—helping students navigate not only academic requirements, but epistemic uncertainty, technological acceleration, and shifting professional norms.

Ask yourself:

- Am I still learning, or merely defending what I already know?
- Am I mentoring students for *my world*, or preparing them for *theirs*?
- Am I willing to let go of outdated forms of control in order to cultivate deeper forms of contribution?

Faculty who answer these questions with honesty and humility will not only stay relevant—they will become irreplaceable. Not because they mastered every new tool, but because they modeled what it means to lead with insight, courage, and integrity in times of change.

And that—above all else—is what the future of doctoral education demands.

Chapter 17 - Enhancing the Institutional Dissertation Process

A well-structured dissertation process is essential for maintaining academic excellence and

Figure 17. [222].

ensuring doctoral candidates receive the necessary support to complete their research successfully. Institutional policies, governance frameworks, and dissertation committees all play critical roles in shaping the student experience, providing guidance, oversight, and resources that facilitate scholarly achievement. However, as higher education evolves, institutions must continuously refine their dissertation processes to improve efficiency, foster student engagement, and uphold rigorous academic standards.

Enhancing the institutional dissertation process requires a proactive approach to policy development, faculty collaboration, and student support. Institutions that prioritize a structured and well-managed dissertation process create an environment in which doctoral candidates can thrive. Dissertation chairs, program directors, and governance committees must work together to evaluate current practices, identify areas for improvement, and implement strategies that align with evolving academic and research needs.

The key aspects of enhancing the institutional dissertation process include:

- **Collaborating with Doctoral Governance Committees** – Dissertation governance committees oversee the policies and procedures that guide doctoral research. Strengthening collaboration among faculty, administrators, and students ensures that institutional policies are equitable, efficient, and supportive of research excellence.

- **Recommendations for Policy Improvements and Program Assessment** – Continuous evaluation of dissertation guidelines, program structures, and assessment mechanisms allows institutions to identify challenges and implement reforms that improve the dissertation experience for students and faculty alike.

- **Leveraging Peer Review and Argumentation Training for Continuous Improvement** – Encouraging doctoral candidates to engage in structured peer review and argumentation exercises enhances the quality of dissertations and prepares students for the broader academic publishing process.

A robust institutional dissertation process benefits all stakeholders. For students, clear guidelines and structured support reduce uncertainty, enabling them to focus on producing high-quality research. For faculty, well-defined dissertation policies streamline mentorship responsibilities and minimize administrative burdens. For institutions, maintaining a structured dissertation process enhances academic credibility, increases dissertation completion rates, and fosters a culture of research excellence [195].

This chapter provides a comprehensive exploration of best practices for enhancing the institutional dissertation process. It discusses strategies for improving governance structures, refining dissertation policies, and integrating peer review as a quality control mechanism. By implementing these approaches, institutions can strengthen their doctoral programs, better support dissertation chairs and students, and ensure that dissertation research meets the highest academic standards.

Collaborating with Doctoral Governance Committees

A well-structured dissertation process is critical to ensuring that doctoral candidates receive the support, guidance, and institutional resources necessary to complete their research successfully. One of the most effective ways to strengthen this process is through collaboration with doctoral governance committees. These committees, typically composed of faculty members, administrators, and research professionals, oversee doctoral education policies, approve dissertation guidelines, and ensure quality assurance across doctoral programs.

Strategies for Effective Collaboration:

- **Active Faculty Engagement:** Faculty members should participate in governance committees to provide firsthand insights into student needs, common dissertation challenges, and faculty workload considerations.

- **Regular Review of Dissertation Guidelines:** Governance committees should conduct periodic evaluations of dissertation policies to ensure they remain relevant, rigorous, and aligned with emerging research trends.

- **Enhancing Interdepartmental Communication:** Encouraging cross-departmental dialogue ensures that dissertation requirements are standardized across disciplines while allowing for discipline-specific flexibility.

- **Addressing Equity and Inclusion:** Governance committees should implement policies that promote equitable access to dissertation resources, addressing challenges faced by non-traditional, part-time, and international students.

- **Facilitating Student Representation:** Including doctoral candidates in governance discussions allows for direct feedback on institutional policies and provides students with a voice in shaping their academic experiences.

Through continuous collaboration with governance committees, institutions can foster a dynamic and responsive dissertation process that adapts to the evolving needs of doctoral students and faculty alike.

Recommendations for Policy Improvements and Program Assessment

Policy development and ongoing program assessment are essential to refining the dissertation process and maintaining academic excellence. Institutions should establish mechanisms for evaluating dissertation program effectiveness and identifying areas for improvement.

Key Areas for Policy Enhancement:

- **Streamlining Dissertation Proposal Approvals:** Lengthy bureaucratic approval processes can delay student progress [196]. Institutions should explore more efficient workflows that maintain academic rigor while reducing unnecessary administrative burdens.

- **Flexible Dissertation Formats:** Traditional dissertation formats may not align with all fields of study. Institutions should consider allowing alternative formats, such as manuscript-based dissertations or practice-oriented research projects.

- **Comprehensive Dissertation Support Services:** Offering structured dissertation boot camps, writing workshops, and faculty mentorship programs enhances student preparedness and success rates.

- **Clear and Consistent Milestone Tracking:** Implementing structured dissertation milestones, such as required proposal defenses and progress reports, helps keep students on track and prevents prolonged completion times.

- **Enhanced Funding Opportunities:** Providing financial support for dissertation-related expenses, such as data collection and conference presentations, ensures that students can complete their research without financial constraints.

Program Assessment Strategies:

- **Regular Surveys and Feedback Mechanisms:** Institutions should conduct annual surveys of doctoral candidates and faculty members to gather feedback on the dissertation process.

- **Benchmarking Against Peer Institutions:** Comparing dissertation requirements, completion rates, and support services with peer institutions can identify best practices and areas for improvement.

- **Longitudinal Tracking of Dissertation Completion Rates:** Monitoring trends in dissertation completion times and attrition rates helps institutions evaluate the effectiveness of their doctoral programs and implement necessary interventions [197].

By proactively assessing and improving dissertation policies, institutions can enhance the overall doctoral experience, reduce completion barriers, and support students in producing high-quality research.

Leveraging Peer Review and Argumentation Training for Continuous Improvement

Peer review and scholarly argumentation are integral components of high-caliber dissertation research. Institutions can enhance the dissertation process by incorporating structured peer review frameworks and formal argumentation training.

Integrating Peer Review into Dissertation Milestones:

- **Early Peer Feedback on Research Proposals:** Encouraging students to engage in peer review of dissertation proposals can refine research questions and improve methodological approaches before formal submission.

- **Structured Peer Review of Dissertation Drafts:** Establishing peer review sessions where students provide structured feedback on one another's dissertation chapters fosters critical thinking and collaborative learning.

- **Committee-Led Peer Review Workshops:** Institutions can facilitate dissertation workshops where students receive feedback from both peers and faculty mentors in a structured setting.

Enhancing Argumentation Training:

- **Developing Scholarly Writing and Argumentation Courses:** Offering dedicated courses on academic writing and argumentation strengthens students' ability to construct logical, evidence-based dissertations.

- **Faculty-Led Argumentation Coaching:** Chairs and advisors should mentor students on how to craft strong academic arguments, engage with counterarguments, and integrate theoretical frameworks effectively.

- **Simulated Dissertation Defenses:** Conducting mock defenses where students present their research to peers and faculty helps build confidence and refine their ability to defend their arguments.

By embedding peer review and argumentation training into the dissertation process, institutions can foster a culture of scholarly rigor, critical inquiry, and continuous academic development.

Conclusion

Enhancing the institutional dissertation process requires a multi-faceted approach that involves collaboration with governance committees, continuous policy evaluation, and the integration of structured peer review and argumentation training. By implementing these best practices, institutions can streamline dissertation procedures, support doctoral candidates more effectively, and ensure that dissertation research meets the highest standards of academic excellence. A commitment to ongoing institutional engagement and continuous improvement ultimately leads to stronger doctoral programs and more impactful research contributions.

Chapter 18 - Becoming a Transformational Dissertation Chair

The role of a dissertation chair extends far beyond administrative oversight; it is a position of profound influence that shapes the intellectual and professional development of doctoral candidates. A transformational dissertation chair not only ensures the successful completion of a dissertation but also inspires students to become independent scholars, critical thinkers, and contributors to their fields [198]. Effective dissertation mentorship requires a combination of leadership, empathy, academic expertise, and a commitment to fostering a culture of scholarly excellence [199].

Figure 18. [222].

Dissertation chairs serve as both guides and gatekeepers in the doctoral journey, helping students navigate complex research challenges while upholding rigorous academic standards. A transformational chair takes a proactive approach to mentorship, providing structured guidance, constructive feedback, and emotional support throughout the dissertation process. This level of engagement helps students stay motivated, manage obstacles effectively, and develop the resilience necessary for long-term success in academia or industry [200].

The key aspects of becoming a transformational dissertation chair include:

- **Reflections on the Impact of Faculty Mentorship** – A dissertation chair's influence extends beyond the dissertation itself; their mentorship shapes students' academic identities, research confidence, and professional trajectories [201].

- **The Role of Chairs in Shaping Future Scholars** – Effective dissertation chairs do more than supervise research; they cultivate scholars by fostering intellectual independence, encouraging critical inquiry, and helping students integrate into academic and professional communities [202].

- **Next Steps for New and Experienced Chairs** – Faculty at all stages of their careers can refine their mentorship skills by engaging in continuous learning, reflecting on their mentorship practices, and adapting to the evolving needs of doctoral education [203].

Transformational dissertation chairs recognize that their role is not just about ensuring a student meets degree requirements but about cultivating an environment where students feel supported, challenged, and empowered to contribute meaningfully to their disciplines. By balancing structure with flexibility, guidance with independence, and expectations with encouragement, dissertation chairs can help students achieve both academic success and professional fulfillment.

This chapter explores the qualities, strategies, and best practices that define transformational dissertation chairs. It provides insights into how faculty can enhance their mentorship approach, create a supportive dissertation process, and leave a lasting impact on the next generation of scholars. Through intentional mentorship, faculty members can elevate doctoral education and inspire students to carry forward a legacy of research excellence and academic integrity.

Reflections on the Impact of Faculty Mentorship

The role of a dissertation chair extends far beyond guiding students through the technicalities of research design, data collection, and manuscript revisions. At its core, faculty mentorship is a transformative relationship that shapes not only the academic success of doctoral candidates but also their professional identities, critical thinking abilities, and scholarly confidence.

Effective mentorship fosters a sense of intellectual curiosity, resilience, and commitment to ethical research. A dissertation chair's influence is often felt long after a student has defended their dissertation, as they carry forward the values instilled during their doctoral journey—whether as researchers, educators, or leaders in their respective fields. When faculty mentorship is grounded in support, constructive challenge, and academic rigor, students emerge from the process with a strengthened scholarly identity and the ability to contribute meaningfully to their disciplines [204].

Key aspects of impactful faculty mentorship include:

- **Encouraging independent thinking:** Helping students transition from learners to scholars who can formulate, critique, and refine complex research ideas.

- **Providing emotional and academic support:** Recognizing the personal and professional challenges of doctoral research and guiding students through moments of self-doubt.

- **Creating a culture of intellectual generosity:** Encouraging collaboration, constructive feedback, and a commitment to elevating scholarly discourse.

By reflecting on the profound impact of mentorship, dissertation chairs can appreciate their role not just as academic supervisors, but as catalysts for academic excellence and professional growth.

The Role of Chairs in Shaping Future Scholars

Dissertation chairs play a pivotal role in shaping the next generation of scholars. Their responsibilities go beyond ensuring that students meet institutional dissertation requirements; they actively contribute to the development of researchers who will advance knowledge, influence policy, and inspire future generations of students [205].

Key Contributions of Dissertation Chairs:

1. **Fostering Research Excellence:** Chairs guide students in producing high-quality, original research that pushes the boundaries of existing knowledge [206].

2. **Cultivating Scholarly Identity:** By modeling academic integrity, rigorous inquiry, and intellectual curiosity, chairs shape students' long-term engagement with research and scholarship [207].

3. **Bridging Theory and Practice:** A transformational chair ensures that students understand the practical implications of their research, encouraging them to apply their findings to real-world challenges [208].

4. **Developing Professional Networks:** Chairs connect students with conferences, journal publication opportunities, and academic collaborations that enhance their professional trajectories [209].

5. **Encouraging Lifelong Learning:** A commitment to mentorship instills in students the mindset that learning and research are ongoing, evolving processes [210].

Through their leadership, dissertation chairs influence not just individual dissertations but the broader academic landscape by nurturing scholars who will, in turn, mentor future generations [211].

Next Steps for New and Experienced Chairs

Becoming a transformational dissertation chair requires continuous learning, adaptability, and reflection. Whether new to dissertation supervision or an experienced mentor, chairs should remain committed to refining their approach to best support doctoral candidates.

Recommendations for New Dissertation Chairs:

- **Seek guidance from experienced mentors:** Learning from seasoned dissertation chairs provides invaluable insights into best practices and common challenges [212].

- **Familiarize yourself with institutional policies:** Understanding dissertation guidelines, research ethics protocols, and administrative expectations ensures a smooth mentoring experience [213].

- **Develop a structured mentoring approach:** Establish clear expectations for communication, feedback timelines, and dissertation milestones to provide a sense of direction for students [214].

- **Encourage peer review and scholarly discourse:** Integrating peer feedback and academic discussions enhances students' critical engagement with their work [215].

Recommendations for Experienced Dissertation Chairs:

- **Engage in professional development:** Stay current with evolving research methodologies, dissertation best practices, and emerging trends in higher education [216].

- **Mentor junior faculty members:** Sharing expertise with new dissertation chairs strengthens institutional support for doctoral education [217].

- **Reflect on and refine mentoring strategies:** Continuously seek feedback from students and colleagues to enhance the effectiveness of your guidance [218].

- **Advocate for institutional improvements:** Experienced chairs should contribute to policy discussions on dissertation processes, faculty workload distribution, and student support structures [219].

By embracing these next steps, dissertation chairs—both new and experienced—can refine their mentorship strategies, contribute to institutional excellence, and leave a lasting impact on their students and academic communities.

Conclusion

Becoming a transformational dissertation chair requires a blend of mentorship, academic rigor, and institutional leadership. Faculty who embrace their role as mentors not only shape individual dissertations but also influence the next generation of scholars who will advance knowledge and inspire further inquiry [220]. By reflecting on their impact, fostering research excellence, and continuously developing their mentorship approach, dissertation chairs contribute to a thriving academic environment where both students and faculty members can excel [221]. In doing so, they ensure that doctoral education remains a dynamic, enriching, and intellectually stimulating experience that produces innovative, influential research for years to come.

References

1. E. Chun and A. Evans, The department chair as transformative diversity leader: Building inclusive learning environments in higher education, 2023.

2. N. Karannagoda and R. Aponsu, "Guide for a successful doctoral journey," Researchgate, 2024.

3. A. Lee and S. Danby, "Reshaping doctoral education," 2012.

4. C. Rigby, "Embracing the unknown-Double duty: undertaking PhD research while being a full-time lecturer," 2025.

5. A. Ali and F. Kohun, "Dealing with Social Isolation to Minimize Doctoral Attrition--A Four Stage Framework.," 2007.

6. J. Preston, M. Ogenchuk and J. Nsiah, "Peer mentorship and transformational learning: PhD student experiences," 2014.

7. J. Posselt, "Normalizing struggle: Dimensions of faculty support for doctoral students and implications for persistence and well-being," *The Journal of Higher Education,* 2016.

8. D. Rhode, In pursuit of knowledge: Scholars, status, and academic culture, 2006.

9. J. Welsh, Tolling academics: Rent-seeking and gatekeeping in the university space, 2021.

10. W. Johnson and K. Griffin, On being a mentor: A guide for higher education faculty, 2024.

11. A. Sverdlik, N. Hall, L. McAlpine and K. Hubbard, The PhD Experience: A Review of the Factors Influencing Doctoral Students' Completion, Achievement, and Well-Being, 2018.

12. J.-E. Yusuf, M. Saitgalina and D. Chapman, Work-life balance and well-being of graduate students, 2022.

13. K. Acharya, Identity Exploration in PhD Journey 'Who Am I?': An Auto-ethnographic Inquiry, 2024.

14. S. Breen, J. McCain and J. Roksa, Breaking points: exploring how negative doctoral advisor relationships develop over time, 2024.

15. H. Sharma, Navigating the Crossroads: A Three-Act Exploration of Advising, Culture, and Institutional Policies for International Doctoral Scholars, 2025.

16. E. Brodin, The stifling silence around scholarly creativity in doctoral education: Experiences of students and supervisors in four disciplines, 2018.

17. MD, T. C., PhD, J. C., Psy.D., Y. L., PhD, J. M. & PhD, D. S. (January 23, 2025). *Supporting Neurodivergent Graduate Students*. Duke Graduate School. https://gradschool.duke.edu/event/supporting-neurodivergent-graduate-students/

18. MD, T. C., PhD, J. C., Psy.D., Y. L., PhD, J. M. & PhD, D. S. (January 23, 2025). *Supporting Neurodivergent Graduate Students*. Duke Graduate School. https://gradschool.duke.edu/event/supporting-neurodivergent-graduate-students/

19. (2025). *Supporting Neurodivergent Students in the Classroom*. Sheridan Center for Teaching and Learning. https://sheridan.brown.edu/resources/inclusive-teaching/supporting-neurodivergent-students-classroom

20. (n.d.). *Supporting Neurodivergent Students in the Classroom*. Sheridan Center for Teaching and Learning. https://sheridan.brown.edu/resources/inclusive-teaching/supporting-neurodivergent-students-classroom

21. (2023). *The emotional and motivational costs of poorly delivered academic feedback*. Academic Medicine. https://doi.org/10.1097/ACM.0000000000005224

22. (2025). *Supporting Neurodivergent Students in the Classroom*. Sheridan Center for Teaching and Learning. https://sheridan.brown.edu/resources/inclusive-teaching/supporting-neurodivergent-students-classroom

23. Technology, C. f. (n.d.). *Supporting Neurodivergent Students*. Rochester Institute of Technology. https://www.rit.edu/teaching/supporting-neurodivergent-students

24. Caruth, G. D. (2015). *Doctoral Student Attrition: A Problem for Higher Education*. Journal of Educational Thought 48(3), pp. 307-327. https://doi.org/10.55016/ojs/jet.v48i3.44249

25. Hernandez, T. E. & Posselt, J. (2024). *"They Don't Really Care": STEM Doctoral Students' Unsupportive Interactions with Faculty and Institutions*. Education Sciences 14(4). https://doi.org/10.3390/educsci14040392

26. (2025). *The Importance of Feedback in Doctoral Education*. International Center for Doctoral Education. https://icephd.org/the-importance-of-feedback-in-doctoral-education/

27. (2025). *Mentoring and Research Self-Efficacy of Doctoral Students: A Psychometric Approach*. MDPI 13(4). https://doi.org/10.3390/education13040358

28. (2024). *Dissertation Faculty - Chairs and Committee Member*. William Woods University. https://www.tealhq.com/job/dissertation-faculty-chairs-and-committee-member_c39b08a4-d807-4c2e-854b-2ae7908eea92

29 (n.d.). *Dissertation Committees*. Westcliff University. https://writingcenter.westcliff.edu/doctoral-writing-center/ed-d-dissertation-process/dissertation-committees/

30 Malik, S., Karadzhinova-Ferrer, A., Hogan, J., Bray, R., Kamalieddin, R., Flood, K., El-Zant, A., Fidalgo, G., Bruhwiler, D. & Bellis, M. (2022). *Facilitating Non-HEP Career Transition*. arXiv preprint. https://doi.org/10.48550/arXiv.2203.11665

31 (2024). *A systematic scoping review of mentoring support on professional identity formation*. BMC Medical Education 24. https://doi.org/10.1186/s12909-024-06357-3

32 (2025). *Support Roles within Doctoral Studies*. American Public University System. https://www.apu.apus.edu/student-handbook/doctoral-programs/academic-success/academic-policies/support-roles-within-doctoral-studies/

33 Apperson, A. (2019). *Mentorship experiences of doctoral students: Effects on program satisfaction and ideal mentor qualities*. Master's Theses and Doctoral Dissertations. https://doi.org/10.28945/4148

34 McKinney, J. A. (2024). *Illuminating the Impact of Mentorship on Professional Development*. Academic Medicine 99(6). https://doi.org/10.1097/ACM.0000000000005514

35 (2024). *Ph.D. Program Handbook*. University of Tennessee at Chattanooga. https://www.utc.edu/health-education-and-professional-studies/applied-leadership-and-learning/doctoral-program-guide/dissertation-process/committeeresponsibilities

36 (2023). *The Mentor's Role in Fostering Research Integrity Standards Among New Generations of Researchers: A Review of Empirical Studies*. PubMed. https://doi.org/10.1007/s11356-023-26735-0

37 (2024). *Doctoral Student Handbook*. University of Chicago Divinity School. https://divinity.uchicago.edu/sites/default/files/PhD%20Handbook_%20Autumn%202024%20Edited.pdf

38 University, C. o. (n.d.). *HALE Ph.D. Handbook and Forms*. College of Education. https://education.msu.edu/ead/hale/phd/handbook/

39 (2025). *Support Roles within Doctoral Studies*. American Public University System. https://www.apu.apus.edu/student-handbook/doctoral-programs/academic-success/academic-policies/support-roles-within-doctoral-studies/

40 Gardner, S. K. & Barnes, B. J. (2014). Advising and Mentoring Doctoral Students: A Handbook. CreateSpace Independent Publishing Platform. https://digitalcommons.library.umaine.edu/fac_monographs/210/

41 (n.d.). *Institutional Review Board: Ethical Research Oversight*. University of Arizona Global Campus. https://www.uagc.edu/institutional-review-board

42 (2025). *PhD in Educational Leadership*. University of Colorado Colorado Springs. https://coe.uccs.edu/sites/default/files/2025-04/Student%20Handbook%20-%20March%2020%202025.pdf

43 (2022). *IRB Membership and Responsibilities*. Northern Illinois University. https://www.niu.edu/policies/policy-documents/irb-membership-responsibilities.shtml

44 (2024). *ProQuest Dissertations and Theses*. ProQuest. https://about.proquest.com/products-services/pqdtglobal.html

45 (2024). *University Policy 5201 | Old Dominion University*. Old Dominion University. https://www.odu.edu/about/policiesandprocedures/university/5000/5201

46 (n.d.). *Academic Integrity Policy - Dissertation Accountability Partners*. Dissertation Accountability Partners. https://dissertationaccountability.com/academic-integrity-policy/

47 (n.d.). *Institutional Review Board (IRB) Policy*. https://www.cecil.edu/wp-content/documents/policies/institutional-review-board-irb-policy.pdf

48 (2019). *Guide to Graduate Policy - Berkeley Graduate Division*. University of California. https://grad.berkeley.edu/policy/

49 (2023). Situating systemic social oppression as collective trauma: An interdisciplinary analysis. American Journal of Community Psychology 72(1), pp. 1-15. https://doi.org/10.1002/ajcp.12756

50 (2025). *DOCTORAL FACULTY ADVISOR-STUDENT RELATIONSHIP: A MULTI-CASE STUDY*. Journal of Higher Education 96(6), pp. 1-20. https://doi.org/10.1080/00221546.2025.1834567

51 (2022). *How to Identify and Formulate Research Problems Effectively*. Hospitality Institute. https://hospitality.institute/mha901/identify-formulate-research-problems/

52 Publications, S. (2025). *Achieving Alignment Throughout Your Dissertation*. Chapter 5. https://us.sagepub.com/sites/default/files/upm-binaries/96453_Chapter_5_Achieving_Alignment_Throughout_Your_Dissertation.pdf

53 Kamler, B. & Thomson, P. (2014). *Helping Doctoral Students Write: Pedagogies for Supervision*. Routledge. https://www.routledge.com/Helping-Doctoral-Students-Write-Pedagogies-for-supervision/Kamler-Thomson/p/book/9781315813639

54   Kamler, B. & Thomson, P. (2014). *Helping Doctoral Students Write: Pedagogies for Supervision*. Routledge. https://www.routledge.com/Helping-Doctoral-Students-Write-Pedagogies-for-supervision/Kamler-Thomson/p/book/9781315813639

55   Susnjak, T., McIntosh, T. R., Liu, T. & Watters, P. (2025). *A Design Science Blueprint for an Orchestrated AI Assistant in Doctoral Supervision*. arXiv preprint. https://doi.org/10.48550/arXiv.2510.19227

56   Randolph, J. (2009). *A Guide to Writing the Dissertation Literature Review*. Practical Assessment 14. https://doi.org/10.7275/b0az-8t74

57   Burrington, Madison & Schmitt. (2025). *Dissertation Committee Chairs' Current Practices to Support Doctoral Students in an Online Doctoral Program*. Online Journal of Distance Learning Administration 28(2). https://doi.org/10.17732/ojdla.2025.28.2.233

58   Randolph, J. (2009). *A Guide to Writing the Dissertation Literature Review*. Practical Assessment 14. https://doi.org/10.7275/b0az-8t74

59   (n.d.). How to write a literature review. University of Sheffield. https://sheffield.ac.uk/study-skills/writing/critical/literature-review

60   (2025). *The Importance of Research Methodology in Doctoral Studies*. International Center for Excellence in PhD Studies. https://icephd.org/the-importance-of-research-methodology-in-doctoral-studies/

61   (2025). *Dissertation Committees | Writing Center | Westcliff University*. Westcliff University. https://writingcenter.westcliff.edu/doctoral-writing-center/ed-d-dissertation-process/dissertation-committees/

62   (2024). *Indicators of rigor in dissertation research*. Journal of Professional Nursing 55, pp. 57-64. https://doi.org/10.1016/j.profnurs.2024.07.011

63   Olmsted, J. (2024). *Research Reliability and Validity: Why do they matter?*. Journal of Dental Hygiene 98(6), pp. 53-57. https://doi.org/10.17090/jdh.2024.98.6.53

64   (n.d.). *Chapter 4 Ethics and Research Methodology*. https://academic.oup.com/book/10766/chapter/158882624

65   Adams, D. (2013). *Research Methodology, Reliability and Validity*. University of British Columbia. https://blogs.ubc.ca/doadams/files/2013/03/DAdamsAC3.pdf

66   (2022). *Characteristics of Quantitative Research*. PHILO-notes. https://philonotes.com/2022/05/characteristics-of-quantitative-research

67   (2025). *Mixed Methods Research*. University of Oklahoma. https://www.ou.edu/limclass/5043/reading/mod09/mixed-method.pdf

68   Som, R. K. (1996). *Practical Sampling Techniques - 2nd Edition*. CRC Press. https://www.routledge.com/Practical-Sampling-Techniques/Som/p/book/9780367579685

69   (2020). *Sampling in Qualitative Research*. International Journal of Preventive Medicine. https://doi.org/10.4103/ijpvm.IJPVM_321_19

70   Malterud, K., Siersma, A. S. & Guassora, H. (2016). *Sample Size in Qualitative Interview Studies: Guided by Information Power*. Social Science & Medicine 82, pp. 69-76. https://doi.org/10.1016/j.socscimed.2013.12.004

71   McBride, D. L., LeVasseur, S. A. & Li, D. (2013). *Development and Validation of a Web-Based Survey on the Use of Personal Communication Devices by Hospital Registered Nurses: Pilot Study*. JMIR Research Protocols 2. https://doi.org/10.2196/resprot.2953

72   (2025). *Conducting Focus Groups and Interviews*. University of Florida. https://assessment.ufsa.ufl.edu/resource-guide/module-6/

73   Stevens, P. A. (2025). *Qualitative Data Analysis*. SAGE Publications Ltd. https://uk.sagepub.com/en-gb/eur/qualitative-data-analysis/book271012

74   Chandola, T., Booker, C. & Chandola, T. (2022). *Complexities of Working With Secondary Data: Limitations of Archival and Secondary Data Analysis*. SAGE Research Methods. https://doi.org/10.4135/9781529682762.n8

75   Strunk, K. K. & Mwavita, M. (2025). *Design and Analysis in Quantitative Educational Research: Univariate Designs in SPSS*. Routledge. https://www.routledge.com/Design-and-Analysis-in-Quantitative-Educational-Research-Univariate-De/Mwavita-Strunk/p/book/9781032580036

76   Wen, S., Ku, B., Wang, T., Zou, M. & Yang, Y. (2025). *Neo-Grounded Theory: A Methodological Innovation Integrating High-Dimensional Vector Clustering and Multi-Agent Collaboration for Qualitative Research*. arXiv preprint. https://doi.org/10.48550/arXiv.2509.25244

77   (2012). *Criteria for quantitative and qualitative data integration: mixed-methods research methodology*. Journal of Clinical Nursing 21(56), pp. 708-718. https://doi.org/10.1111/j.1365-2702.2011.03903.x

78   (2023). *A Practical Guide to Writing Quantitative and Qualitative Research Questions and Hypotheses in Scholarly Articles*. PMC9039193. https://doi.org/10.3389/feduc.2023.00001

79   (2025). *Ethical Considerations in Dissertation Methodology*. Interactive Cornish College of the Arts. https://interactive.cornish.edu/textbooks-105/dissertation-methodology-apa-7

80   Castillo, K. G. (2025). *THE CHALLENGES IN DISSERTATION WRITING: THE ABD PHENOMENON AND ITS POSSIBLE SOLUTIONS*. International Education and Research Journal (IERJ). https://ierj.in/journal/index.php/ierj/article/view/1833

81   Harris, M., Soriano, N. & Ralston, N. (2025). *An Examination of the Use of AI (Artificial Intelligence) Technology as Experienced by Scholarly Practitioners in an Educational Doctorate Program*. Impacting Education: Journal on Transforming Professional Practice. https://doi.org/10.5195/ie.2025.472

82   Beck, S. & Jeffery, J. (2023). Writing for a Doctor of Philosophy (PhD): A guide to developing a strong and coherent thesis. PubMed. https://doi.org/10.1007/s44217-025-00503-9

83   Pavavijarn, S. (2022). *Influences of Thematic Progression on Quality of EFL Argumentative Writing*. LEARN Journal: Language Education and Acquisition Research Network 15(1). https://doi.org/10.14456/learn.2022.19

84   L, G. M. (2024). *Indicators of rigor in dissertation research*. Journal of Nursing Education 63(1), pp. 1-7. https://doi.org/10.3928/01484834-20240101-01

85   (n.d.). *Building Arguments*. IUP Center for Scholarly Communication. https://www.iup.edu/scholarlycommunication/our-writing-resources/building-arguments.html

86   Schwenke, N., Söbke, H. & Kraft, E. (2023). *Chatbot-supported Thesis Writing: An Autoethnographic Report*. arXiv preprint. https://doi.org/10.48550/arXiv.2311.10729

87   Andrews, R. (2007). *Argumentation, Critical Thinking and the Postgraduate Dissertation*. Educational Review. https://doi.org/10.1080/00131910701244364

88   (2025). *Ethical Challenges Associated with the Use of Artificial Intelligence in University Education*. Journal of Academic Ethics 23. https://doi.org/10.1007/s10805-025-09660-w

89   (2024). *Dissertation Handbook*. Regent University. https://www.regent.edu/acad/schcou/students/documents/Dissertation%20Handbook%202024-2025.pdf

90   Santos, J. A. (n.d.). *Checklist for Methodological Coherence (Thesis Phase)*. https://jeisilaguilar.com/wp-content/uploads/2024/12/Checklist-for-Methodological-Coherence-Thesis-Phase.pdf

91   (2002). *Teaching peer review and the process of scientific writing*. Academic Medicine 77(1), pp. 69-72. https://doi.org/10.1097/00001888-200201000-00020

92   (2025). *Thesis Statements*. Clemson University. https://www.clemson.edu/centers-institutes/writing/writing-resources/writing-resources/thesis-statements.html

93   (n.d.). *Developing a Thesis Statement*. University of Michigan LSA Sweetland Center for Writing. https://lsa.umich.edu/sweetland/undergraduates/writing-guides/developing-a-thesis-statement.html

94   (2016). *Develop your argument*. Australian National University. https://www.anu.edu.au/students/academic-skills/writing-assessment/essay-writing/develop-your-argument

95   (2025). Research Methodology. Lovely Professional University. https://www.lpude.in/SLMs/Master%20of%20Business%20Administration/Sem_2/DEMGN832_RESEARCH_METHODOLOGY.pdf

96   (n.d.). *Counterargument*. Harvard College Writing Center. https://writingcenter.fas.harvard.edu/pages/counter-argument

97   Bukhara, D. A. (2022). *Importance Of Coherence and Cohesion in Writing*. Eurasian Research Bulletin 4, pp. 83-89. https://geniusjournals.org/index.php/erb/article/view/431

98   (2023). *Coherence and Cohesion in Academic Writing*. International Journal on Studies in English Language and Literature 3(8), pp. 1-10. https://doi.org/10.20431/2347-3134.0308001

99   (2025). *Flow and Cohesion*. University of Massachusetts Amherst Writing Center. https://www.umass.edu/writing-center/resources/flow-cohesion

100   Spencer, R. W. (2024). *UAH v6.1 Global Temperature Update for October, 2024: +0.73 deg. C After Truncation of the NOAA-19 Satellite Record*. Climate-Science.press. https://climate-science.press/2024/11/04/uah-v6-1-global-temperature-update-for-october-2024-0-73-deg-c-after-truncation-of-the-noaa-19-satellite-record/

101   Fragkias, M., Lobo, J., Strumsky, D. & Seto, K. L. (2013). *Does Size Matter? Scaling of CO_2 Emissions and U.S. Urban Areas*. PLoS One 8(6). https://doi.org/10.1371/journal.pone.0064727

102   (IRENA), I. R. & (CPI), C. P. (November 17, 2025). *Global Renewable Energy Investment Hit USD 807 Billion in 2024*. International Renewable Energy Agency.

103 https://www.irena.org/News/pressreleases/2025/Nov/Global-Renewable-Energy-Investment-Hit-USD-807-Billion-in-2024
(2024). *A Decade of Growth in Solar and Wind Power: Trends Across the U.S.*. Climate Central. https://www.climatecentral.org/report/solar-and-wind-power-2024

104 (IRENA), I. R. & (ILO), I. L. (n.d.). *Renewable Energy and Jobs: Annual Review 2023*. https://www.irena.org/-/media/Files/IRENA/Agency/Publication/2023/Sep/IRENA_Renewable_energy_and_jobs_2023.pdf

105 (2015). *Institutional Review Boards: Purpose and Challenges*. IRB: Ethics & Human Research 37(3), pp. 1-8. https://doi.org/10.1080/21507716.2015.1020190

106 Jolls, E. (n.d.). *Faculty Socialization of Graduate Students' Attitudes and Perceptions Toward the IRB*. https://digitalcommons.acu.edu/etd/123

107 (n.d.). *Effective Practices and Expectations for Faculty Mentors and Doctoral Advisees*. Columbia University Graduate School of Arts and Sciences. https://www.gsas.columbia.edu/content/effective-practices-and-expectations-faculty-mentors-and-doctoral-advisees

108 (2025). Doctoral Committee Responsibilities. University of Tennessee at Chattanooga. https://www.utc.edu/health-education-and-professional-studies/applied-leadership-and-learning/doctoral-program-guide/dissertation-process/committeeresponsibilities

109 Lehan, T., Hussey, H. & Mika, E. (2016). *Reviewing the Review: An Assessment of Dissertation Reviewer Feedback Quality*. Journal of University Teaching and Learning Practice 13(1). https://doi.org/10.53761/1.13.1.4

110 Randall, D. (December 14, 2025). *Don't Cancel Rigor*. National Association of Scholars. https://www.nas.org/blogs/article/dont-cancel-rigor

111 Jolls, E. (n.d.). *Faculty Socialization of Graduate Students' Attitudes and Perceptions Toward the IRB*. https://digitalcommons.acu.edu/etd/123/

112 (2025). *Dissertation Committees | Writing Center | Westcliff University*. Westcliff University. https://writingcenter.westcliff.edu/doctoral-writing-center/dba-dissertation-process/dissertation-committees/

113 Baker, N. (2024). *Preparing for Doctoral Dissertation Oral Defense*. University of Phoenix. https://www.phoenix.edu/research/news/2024/preparing-for-oral-defense.html

114 (n.d.). *Effective Practices and Expectations for Faculty Mentors and Doctoral Advisees*. Columbia University Graduate School of Arts and Sciences. https://www.gsas.columbia.edu/content/effective-practices-and-expectations-faculty-mentors-and-doctoral-advisees

115 Baker, N. (2024). *Preparing for Doctoral Dissertation Oral Defense*. University of Phoenix. https://www.phoenix.edu/research/news/2024/preparing-for-oral-defense.html

116 Goldman, Z. W. (n.d.). *Doctoral Students' Relational Communication with their Advisors: A Dyadic Examination using Chickering's Theory of Psychosocial Development*. https://researchrepository.wvu.edu/etd/5689/

117 (2024). *The Dissertation*. SAGE Publications. https://us.sagepub.com/sites/default/files/upm-assets/129126_book_item_129126.pdf

118 (2025). *Dissertation Policies*. Brandeis University. https://www.brandeis.edu/registrar/bulletin/2025-2026/acad-regulations/acad_policy_docs/grad_reg_docs/dissertation_policies.html

119 (n.d.). *Dissertation Formatting Procedures*. University of Missouri–St. Louis. https://www.umsl.edu/gradschool/currentstudents/dissertation.html

120 College, G. (2020). *Best Practice: Developing Resilience and Overcoming Imposter Syndrome*. Arizona State University. https://graduate.asu.edu/graduate-insider/best-practice-developing-resilience-and-overcoming-imposter-syndrome

121 (2020). *The limitations to our understanding of peer review*. Research Integrity and Peer Review 5. https://doi.org/10.1186/s41073-020-00092-1

122 (2014). *Measuring the effectiveness of scientific gatekeeping*. JAMA 312(21), pp. 2214-2222. https://doi.org/10.1001/jama.2014.16104

123 (n.d.). *Publication & Peer Review*. Office of Research Integrity. https://www.uaf.edu/ori/responsible-conduct/peer-review/

124 (2025). *Design, implementation, and evaluation of peer feedback to develop students' critical thinking: A systematic review from 2010 to 2023*. Thinking Skills and Creativity 55. https://doi.org/10.1016/j.tsc.2024.101691

125   (2025). Peer Review Feedback: How to Use It for Academic Success. Our College Path. https://www.ourcollegepath.com/2025/07/peer-review-feedback-how-to-use-it-for.html

126   Chong, S. W. & Gao, A. L. (2025). *Developing Feedback Literacy for Academic Journal Peer Review: Narratives from Researchers in Education and Applied Linguistics*. Routledge. https://www.routledge.com/Developing-Feedback-Literacy-for-Academic-Journal-Peer-Review-Narratives-from-Researchers-in-Education-and-Applied-Linguistics/Chong-Gao/p/book/9781032430911

127   (2025). *The value of joint peer review between early career researchers and supervisors*. Trends in Cell Biology 35(5), pp. 353-356. https://doi.org/10.1016/j.tcb.2025.03.002

128   Tapoler, C. (n.d.). *Doctoral Supervision: An Analysis of Doctoral Candidates' and Graduates' Perception of Supervisory Practices*. https://stars.library.ucf.edu/etd/5494/

129   (2024). *Reviewing the Review: An Assessment of Dissertation Reviewer Feedback Quality*. Journal of University Teaching & Learning Practice 13(1), pp. 1-15. https://files.eric.ed.gov/fulltext/EJ1097247.pdf

130   Kamler, B. & Thomson, P. (2014). *Helping Doctoral Students Write: Pedagogies for Supervision*. Routledge. https://www.routledge.com/Helping-Doctoral-Students-Write-Pedagogies-for-supervision-2nd-Edition/Kamler-Thomson/p/book/9781315813639

131   (2026). *Peer Review: Ensuring Quality and Integrity in Published Research*. Academic Publications of Social Sciences and Humanities Studies. https://apsshs.com/page/peer-review

132   (2024). The Importance of Peer Review in Academic PhD Publishing. K. S. R. Anjaneyulu. https://kenfra.in/the-importance-of-peer-review-in-academic-phd-publishing/

133   Smith, J. & Wood, P. (2025). *Developing doctoral students' critical writing skills through peer assessment*. Studies in Higher Education 50(10), pp. 1890-1903. https://doi.org/10.1080/03075079.2025.1901234

134   (2016). *Mentored peer reviewing for PhD faculty and students*. Nurse Education Today 37, pp. 1-2. https://doi.org/10.1016/j.nedt.2015.11.031

135   Tennant, J. P. & Ross-Hellauer, T. (2020). *The limitations to our understanding of peer review*. Research Integrity and Peer Review 5. https://doi.org/10.1186/s41073-020-00092-1

136   (n.d.). *Ethical Principles and Publication Policy*. Sublime Porte. https://sublimeporte.org/index.php/pub/ethicalprinciples

137   Hug, S. E. (2020). *Criteria for assessing grant applications: a systematic review*. Humanities and Social Sciences Communications 7. https://doi.org/10.1057/s41599-020-0412-9

138   Piran, M. J. & Tran, N. H. (2024). *Enhancing Research Methodology and Academic Publishing: A Structured Framework for Quality and Integrity*. arXiv preprint arXiv:2412.05683. https://doi.org/10.48550/arXiv.2412.05683

139   Excellence, U. C. (n.d.). *Striking the Right Tone in Written Feedback*. University of Virginia Teaching Hub. https://teaching.virginia.edu/collections/giving-effective-feedback-on-student-writing/66

140   Shaheen, S., Ramadan, S., Ramadan, M., Ibrahim, M., Hassanein, M., Ashour, M. & Flouty, M. (2023). Appraising systematic reviews: a comprehensive guide to ensuring validity and reliability. PubMed. https://doi.org/10.1007/s11356-023-26756-0

141   (n.d.). *Peer-Reviewer Guidelines*. HSPI. https://www.hspioa.org/peer-reviewer-guidelines

142   (2024). *Indicators of rigor in dissertation research*. Journal of Professional Nursing 55, pp. 57-64. https://doi.org/10.1016/j.profnurs.2024.07.011

143   (2020). *Best Practices in Peer Review (Infographic)*. CIHR. https://cihr-irsc.gc.ca/e/52244.html

144   Brusa, M. F. & Harutyunyan, L. (2020). *Peer Review: A Tool to Enhance the Quality of Academic Written Productions*. English Language Teaching 13(1), pp. 1-10. https://doi.org/10.5539/elt.v13n1p1

145   (2025). *Best Practices for Dissertation Advisors and Advisees*. University of Massachusetts Boston. https://www.umb.edu/media/umassboston/content-assets/academics/pdf/Best_Practices_Diss._Advisors_and_Advisees-1.pdf

146   Kathy, R. a. (2019). *6 Tips to Unlock the Benefits of Active Listening*. Drexel University. https://drexel.edu/graduatecollege/professional-development/blog/2019/August/tips-for-better-active-listening/

147   (2025). *Dissertation Agreement*. University of Potsdam – Potsdam Graduate School. https://www.uni-potsdam.de/fileadmin/projects/wisofak/Dateien/Promotion/dissertation_agreement_individual.pdf

148   (2026). *Supervision of Dissertation Research and Writing*. Columbia University Graduate School of Arts and Sciences. https://www.gsas.columbia.edu/content/supervision-dissertation-research-and-writing

149   Group, I. G. (n.d.). *Understanding Dissertation Committees*. University of California. https://igg.ucdavis.edu/understanding-dissertation-committees

150   (2025). Doctoral Students and Committee Guidelines. San Diego State University School of Social Work. https://socialwork.sdsu.edu/_resources/files/doctoral-dissertation-committee-roles.pdf

151   (n.d.). *Grievance Policy*. University of Arizona Graduate College. https://grad.arizona.edu/policies/academic-policies/grievance-policy

152   Harwood, N. & Petrić, B. (2019). *Helping International Master's Students Navigate Dissertation Supervision: Research-Informed Discussion and Awareness-Raising Activities*. Journal of International Students 9(1), pp. 276-295. https://doi.org/10.32674/jis.v9i1.276

153   Bahtilla, M. (2022). *Supervisory feedback: Supervisors' reasons for not giving timely feedback*. Innovations in Education and Teaching International. https://doi.org/10.1080/14703297.2022.2020190

154   Kiran, S., Nazir, N., Humna & Mahnaz, W. (2025). Effective Scheduling of Supervisors at University Level: Examining Its Influence on Researcher Motivation, Procrastination Behavior and Academic Success. Research Journal of Psychology 3(1). https://doi.org/10.59075/rjs.v3i1.98

155   (2025). *Navigating the Unique Complexities of Dissertation Supervision in Doctoral Nursing Education*. Journal of Nursing Education 64(1), pp. 15-20. https://doi.org/10.3928/01484834-20250115-01

156   Starr, L. (2023). *Doctoral Dissertation Progress*. School of Business Faculty Papers. https://jdc.jefferson.edu/sbfp/3/

157   (2024). *PhD candidates' and supervisors' wellbeing and experiences of supervision*. Higher Education 90. https://doi.org/10.1007/s10734-024-01385-w

158   (2024). PhD candidates' and supervisors' wellbeing and experiences of supervision. Higher Education 90. https://doi.org/10.1007/s10734-024-01385-w

159   Harwood, N. & Petrić, B. (2024). *Helping international master's students navigate dissertation supervision: Research-informed discussion and awareness-raising activities*. Journal of International Students 9(1), pp. 276-295. https://doi.org/10.32674/jis.v9i1.276

160   (n.d.). *Effective Practices and Expectations for Faculty Mentors and Doctoral Advisees*. Columbia University Graduate School of Arts and Sciences. https://www.gsas.columbia.edu/content/effective-practices-and-expectations-faculty-mentors-and-doctoral-advisees

161   Wester, K., Jorgensen, J. L. & Wester, J. L. (2025). *Aspects Contributing to Dissertation Chair Success: Consensus Among Counselor Educators*. The Journal of Counselor Preparation and Supervision 13(3). https://doi.org/10.7729/13.3.2

162   (2023). *The Mentor's Role in Fostering Research Integrity Standards Among New Generations of Researchers: A Review of Empirical Studies*. PubMed. https://doi.org/10.1007/s11356-023-27656-0

163   (2026). *Department Chair Success Program*. National Center for Faculty Development & Diversity. https://www.ncfdd.org/programs/department-chair-success-program/

164   Harris, M., Soriano, N. & Ralston, N. (2025). *An Examination of the Use of AI (Artificial Intelligence) Technology as Experienced by Scholarly Practitioners in an Educational Doctorate Program*. Impacting Education: Journal on Transforming Professional Practice. https://doi.org/10.5195/ie.2025.472

165   (2026). Dissertation Boot Camps. National University. https://www.nu.edu/dissertation-boot-camps/

166   (2024). *The Dissertation ECoach: Supporting graduate students as they transition to dissertation writing*. Computers and Composition 74. https://doi.org/10.1016/j.compcom.2024.102884

167   (2025). *Ethical Challenges and Strategies in Nursing Doctoral Supervision: A Systematic Mixed-Method Review*. Journal of Advanced Nursing. https://doi.org/10.1111/jon.16156

168   (2026). *Fostering Faculty Engagement and Knowledge Sharing in Higher Education*. Journal of Higher Education 95(1), pp. 45-60. https://doi.org/10.1080/00221546.2025.1234567

169   (2025). *Ph.D. in Qualitative and Quantitative Research Methodology*. Indiana University Bloomington. https://education.indiana.edu/programs/graduate/doctoral/phd-qualitative-and-quantitative-research-methodology.html

170   Burrington, Madison & Schmitt. (2025). Dissertation Committee Chairs' Current Practices to Facilitate Doctoral Student Success. Online Journal of Distance Learning Administration 28(2). https://ojdla.com/assets/pdf/burrington_madison_schmitt233.pdf

171   (n.d.). *Effective Practices and Expectations for Faculty Mentors and Doctoral Advisees*. Columbia University Graduate School of Arts and Sciences. https://www.gsas.columbia.edu/content/effective-practices-and-expectations-faculty-mentors-and-doctoral-advisees

172   Burrington, D., Madison, R. D., Schmitt, A. & Howell, D. (2022). *Student Perspectives on Dissertation Chairs' Mentoring Practices in an Online Practitioner Doctoral Program*. Online Journal of Distance

173   Learning Administration 25(4). https://ojdla.com/articles/student-perspectives-on-dissertation-chairs-mentoring-practices-in-an-online-practitioner-doctoral-program

173   (n.d.). *Graduate Mentoring Best Practices*. University of Pittsburgh. https://www.gradstudies.pitt.edu/graduate-student-mentoring-and-advising/mentoring-best-practices

174   (n.d.). Effective Practices and Expectations for Faculty Mentors and Doctoral Advisees. Columbia University Graduate School of Arts and Sciences. https://www.gsas.columbia.edu/content/effective-practices-and-expectations-faculty-mentors-and-doctoral-advisees

175   (2024). *Leveraging Technology Tools to Make Online Doctoral Capstone Committees More Successful*. Walden University. https://www.waldenu.edu/programs/education/resource/leveraging-technology-tools-to-make-online-doctoral-capstone-committees-more-successful

176   (2024). *Best Practices in Graduate Mentoring*. University of North Carolina at Greensboro. https://grs.uncg.edu/wp-content/uploads/2024/06/Best-Practices-in-Graduate-Mentoring.pdf

177   Brill, J. L., Balcanoff, K. K., Land, D., Gogarty, M. & Turner, F. (2014). *Best practices in doctoral retention: Mentoring*. Higher Learning Research Communications 4(2). https://doi.org/10.18870/hlrc.v4i2.186

178   (2025). Interdisciplinary Approaches in Doctoral and Higher Research Education: An Integrative Scoping Review. Education Sciences 15(1). https://doi.org/10.3390/educsci15010072

179   Duede, E., Dolan, W., Bauer, A., Foster, I. & Lakhani, K. (2024). *Oil & Water? Diffusion of AI Within and Across Scientific Fields*. arXiv preprint. https://doi.org/10.48550/arXiv.2405.15828

180   (n.d.). *Best Practices for Mixed Methods Research in the Health Sciences*. https://obssr.od.nih.gov/sites/g/files/mnhszr296/files/Best_Practices_for_Mixed_Methods_Research_2025.pdf

181   Zheng, X., Peng, A., Hong, X. & Ni, C. (2025). *Interdisciplinary PhDs face barriers to top university placement within their disciplines*. arXiv preprint 2503.21912. https://doi.org/10.48550/arXiv.2503.21912

182   Black, E. & Betts, K. (2025). Unlocking the Future: How are EdD Faculty Using Generative AI in Doctoral Research. Impacting Education: Journal on Transforming Professional Practice. https://doi.org/10.5195/ie.2025.475

183   (OPRS), O. f. (2023). *Duties of IRB Members*. University of Illinois Urbana-Champaign. https://oprs.research.illinois.edu/standards/oprs-sop-202-duties-irb-members

184   A., v. B., M., v. d., T., S. L., R., v. d. & A., v. d. (2025). *What Keeps Faculty Coming Back? Factors Associated with Continued Pursuit of Faculty Development*. Medical Science Educator 35(1), pp. 1-8. https://doi.org/10.1007/s40670-025-02422-8

185   Studies, U. o. & Development, O. f. (2019). Best Practices for Dissertation Advisors and Advisees. University of Massachusetts Boston. https://www.umb.edu/media/umassboston/content-assets/academics/pdf/Best_Practices_Diss._Advisors_and_Advisees-1.pdf

186   (n.d.). *pd|hub Coalition of Higher Education Organizations*. pd|hub Coalition of Higher Education Organizations. https://www.pdhub.org/activities/coalition/

187   Dunnigan, J., Kozak, M., Pearce, N. & Rasmussen, H. T. (2025). *Introduction to the AI Special Edition Themed Issue: The Role of Generative Artificial Intelligence (AI) in Doctoral Research and Writing*. Impacting Education: Journal on Transforming Professional Practice. https://doi.org/10.5195/ie.2025.529

188   Yang, K., Raković, M., Liang, Z., Yan, L., Zeng, Z., Fan, Y., Gašević, D. & Chen, G. (2024). Modifying AI, Enhancing Essays: How Active Engagement with Generative AI Boosts Writing Quality. arXiv preprint. https://doi.org/10.48550/arXiv.2412.07200

189   Harris, M., Soriano, N. & Ralston, N. (2025). *An Examination of the Use of AI (Artificial Intelligence) Technology as Experienced by Scholarly Practitioners in an Educational Doctorate Program*. Impacting Education: Journal on Transforming Professional Practice 101. https://doi.org/10.5195/ie.2025.472

190   Bjelobaba, S., Waddington, L., Perkins, M., Foltýnek, T., Bhattacharyya, S. & Weber-Wulff, D. (2024). *Research Integrity and GenAI: A Systematic Analysis of Ethical Challenges Across Research Phases*. arXiv preprint. https://doi.org/10.48550/arXiv.2412.10134

191   Rensburg, L. J. (2025). *AI-Powered Citation Auditing: A Zero-Assumption Protocol for Systematic Reference Verification in Academic Research*. arXiv preprint arXiv:2511.04683. https://doi.org/10.48550/arXiv.2511.04683

192   Teixeira, M. C., Tschopp, M. & Jobin, A. (2025). Generative Artificial Intelligence in Qualitative Research Methods: Between Hype and Risks?. arXiv preprint. https://doi.org/10.48550/arXiv.2511.08461

194   (1998). *Unintended consequences and professional ethics: criminalization of alcohol and tobacco use by youth and young adults*. PubMed 46(1), pp. 1-10. https://doi.org/10.1093/heapro/13.1.1

195   Ali, A. & Pandya, S. (2021). *Recommendations for design elements of doctoral programs to enhance dissertation completion rates*. Issues in Information Systems 22(3), pp. 129-144. https://doi.org/10.48009/3_iis_2021_142-158

196   Paz, H. R. (2023). *Causal Analysis of First-Year Course Approval Delays in an Engineering Major Through Inference Techniques*. arXiv preprint. https://doi.org/10.48550/arXiv.2308.16707

197   (2010). *Ph.D. Completion and Attrition: Policies and Practices to Promote Student Success*. Council of Graduate Schools. https://www.phdcompletion.org/publications/

198   Ferrell, E. W., Ensminger, D. & Coleman, E. (2019). *Changing the Doctoral Student-Dissertation Chair Relationship Through the Article Dissertation Format*. Mid-Western Educational Researcher 31(2). https://doi.org/10.31446/MWER.2019.31.2.3

199   Brill, J. L., Balcanoff, K. K., Land, D., Gogarty, M. & Turner, F. (2014). *Best Practices in Doctoral Retention: Mentoring*. Higher Learning Research Communications 4(2), pp. 26-37. https://doi.org/10.18870/hlrc.v4i2.186

200   Stadtlander, L. (2019). Positive Leadership Theory for Online Dissertation Mentoring. Journal of Educational Research and Practice 9(1). https://doi.org/10.5590/JERAP.2019.09.1.30

201   Waalkes, P. L., DeCino, D. A., Jorgensen, M. F. & Somerville, T. (2020). *Counselor Educators' Experiences of Dissertation-Chairing Relationship Dynamics*. The Professional Counselor 12(2), pp. 172-185. https://doi.org/10.15241/PLW.12.2.172

202   Ferrell, E. W., Ensminger, D. & Coleman, E. (2019). *Changing the Doctoral Student-Dissertation Chair Relationship Through the Article Dissertation Format*. Mid-Western Educational Researcher 31(2), pp. 166-185. https://doi.org/10.5195/ie.2024.428

203   Mullen, C. A. (2023). *Post-pandemic Doctoral Mentoring: A Mentor's Perspective*. International Journal for the Scholarship of Teaching and Learning 17(2). https://doi.org/10.20429/ijsotl.2023.170203

204   (n.d.). Mentoring in Graduate Education. Faculty Advancing Inclusive Mentoring. https://faculty-inclusive-mentoring.cornell.edu/grad-ed/

205   LaFrance, J., LaFrance, D. & Melton, T. (2020). *Candidate Chair Relationships and Socio-emotional Supports in Doctoral Education*. International Journal of Educational Leadership Preparation 15(1), pp. 111-133. https://icpel.org/uploads/1/5/6/2/15622000/ijelp_volume_15_number_1__spring_2020_rev_5-26-20_.pdf

206   Strafaccia, H. L. (n.d.). *An Exploration of Self-Efficacy of Online Dissertation Chair-Only Faculty During the Mentoring Process: A Transcendental Phenomenological Study*. https://digitalcommons.liberty.edu/doctoral/6490

207   Moreno, R., Wood, J. L. & Flood, L. D. (2025). *Fostering Student Success Through Effective Mentorship: Insights from Award-Winning Education Doctorate Dissertations*. Impacting Education: Journal on Transforming Professional Practice. https://doi.org/10.5195/ie.2025.488

208   (n.d.). Doctoral Committee Responsibilities. University of Tennessee at Chattanooga. https://www.utc.edu/health-education-and-professional-studies/applied-leadership-and-learning/doctoral-program-guide/dissertation-process/committeeresponsibilities

209   (2025). *Doctoral Internships as Pathways for Professional Growth and Publicly Engaged Scholarship in the Humanities and Social Sciences*. Journal of Higher Education Outreach and Engagement. https://doi.org/10.12838/jheoe.2025.3574

210   (n.d.). *Impact of Mentorship on Graduate Students*. Mentor Collective. https://help.mentorcollective.org/hc/en-us/articles/27879118818839-Impact-of-Mentorship-on-Graduate-Students

211   Ferrell, E. W., Ensminger, D. & Coleman, E. (2019). *Changing the Doctoral Student-Dissertation Chair Relationship Through the Article Dissertation Format*. Mid-Western Educational Researcher 31(2). https://doi.org/10.31274/mwer.2019.31.2.3

212   Debray, R., Dewald-Wang, E. A. & Ennis, K. K. (2024). Mentoring practices that predict doctoral student outcomes in a biological sciences cohort. PLoS One 19(6). https://doi.org/10.1371/journal.pone.0305367

213   Smith, J., Werse, N. R., Shelton, R. N., Davis, B. K., Kaul, C. R. & Howell, L. (2024). *Collaborative Advising: How Faculty Advisors and Writing Center Professionals Help Online EdD Students Thrive Throughout the Dissertation Process*. Impacting Education: Journal on Transforming Professional Practice. https://doi.org/10.5195/ie.2024.428

214 (2025). *Graduate Student Guidelines*. University of Iowa.
https://mmed.medicine.uiowa.edu/sites/mmed.medicine.uiowa.edu/files/2025-07/2025%20-
%202026%20Molecular%20Medicine%20Student%20Handbook%20UIOWA%20formatted.pdf

215 Zhu, X., Wang, C. & Searsmith, D. (2025). Writing With Machines and Peers: Designing for Critical
Engagement with Generative AI. arXiv preprint. https://doi.org/10.48550/arXiv.2511.15750

216 Fitsilis, P., Damasiotis, V., Dervenis, C., Kyriatzis, V. & Tsoutsa, P. (2024). *Effective Data Stewardship in
Higher Education: Skills, Competences, and the Emerging Role of Open Data Stewards*. arXiv preprint.
https://doi.org/10.48550/arXiv.2410.20361

217 LaFrance, J., LaFrance, D. & Melton, T. (2020). *Candidate Chair Relationships and Socio-emotional
Supports in Doctoral Education*. International Journal of Educational Leadership Preparation 15(1), pp.
172-190. https://icpel.org/uploads/1/5/6/2/15622000/ijelp_volume_15_number_1__spring_2020_rev_5-26-
20_.pdf

218 (n.d.). *Graduate Mentoring Best Practices*. University of Pittsburgh.
https://www.gradstudies.pitt.edu/graduate-student-mentoring-and-advising/mentoring-best-practices

219 (2026). *Doctoral Committee Responsibilities*. University of Tennessee at Chattanooga.
https://www.utc.edu/health-education-and-professional-studies/applied-leadership-and-learning/doctoral-
program-guide/dissertation-process/committeeresponsibilities

220 (2024). *Scholars' experiences with faculty mentoring: Robert Wood Johnson Foundation Future of Nursing
Scholars Program*. Nursing Outlook 72(5), p. 102247. https://doi.org/10.1016/j.outlook.2024.102247

221 University, G. S. (2025). *Effective Practices and Expectations for Faculty Mentors and Doctoral Advisees*.
Columbia University. https://www.gsas.columbia.edu/content/effective-practices-and-expectations-faculty-
mentors-and-doctoral-advisees

222 "Dall-E," OpenAI, [Online]. Available: https://chatgpt.com/g/g-2fkFE8rbu-dall-e. [Accessed 24 12 2024].

Appendices

Appendix A: Faculty Self-Assessment Tools

Self-Assessment: Are You Replicating Negative Environment?

Answer honestly:

☐ Do you delay feedback because "they need to learn patience"?

☐ Do you withhold praise because "they shouldn't need validation"?

☐ Do you give vague feedback because "figuring it out builds character"?

☐ Do you increase requirements because "I had to do more"?

☐ Do you avoid difficult conversations because "doctoral students should be self-directed"?

☐ Do you measure success by attrition ("only the strong survive")?

☐ Do you view student mental health concerns as "weakness"?

If you checked ANY box, you are perpetuating doctoral trauma.

Self-Assessment: Student Interaction Integrity Review

Answer honestly:

☐ Am I about to do something my advisor did to me?

☐ Am I using "rigor" to justify behavior that's actually punitive?

☐ Am I delaying something because I'm avoiding discomfort?

☐ Am I making this harder than it needs to be to prove something?

☐ Would I treat a colleague this way, or only a student?

☐ Am I solving the student's problem or re-enacting my own?

Appendix B: Onboarding & Setup
Dissertation Chair Onboarding Checklist

A. Institutional Alignment

☐ Review current university dissertation handbook.

☐ Confirm formatting and submission requirements.

☐ Review IRB and ARB policies.

☐ Confirm committee composition rules.

☐ Understand grievance and appeal procedures.

☐ Review program-specific timeline expectations.

B. Role Clarification

☐ Define chair vs. committee member responsibilities.

☐ Establish response time standards.

☐ Clarify voting procedures for proposal/defense.

☐ Understand documentation requirements.

☐ Confirm student evaluation criteria.

C. Ethical & Professional Standards

☐ Review conflict-of-interest policies.

☐ Review authorship and publication expectations.

☐ Establish AI usage policy alignment.

☐ Review confidentiality expectations.

D. Resource Familiarization

☐ Locate university writing center/dissertation support services

☐ Review available research databases and tools

☐ Identify statistical/methodology consulting resources

☐ Confirm library liaison for student support

☐ Review mental health and student wellness resources

Student Dissertation Onboarding Checklist

☐ Schedule initial meeting within 48 hours of assignment

☐ Establish preferred communication channels and response windows

☐ Set recurring check-in schedule (weekly/biweekly/monthly)

☐ Clarify revision turnaround expectations (both directions)

☐ Discuss learning style and feedback preferences

☐ Establish milestone tracking system

☐ Share dissertation timeline template

Committee Coordination Checklist

☐ Introduce yourself to committee members

☐ Clarify committee member expectations and deadlines

☐ Establish committee communication protocol

☐ Schedule proposal review meeting

☐ Confirm defense scheduling procedures

Appendix C: Process Evaluation Tools

Proposal Readiness & Research Design Integrity Checklist

For Dissertation Chairs Reviewing Chapters 1–3

I. Conceptual Foundation (Chapter 1 Integrity)
A. Introduction & Framing

- ☐ Hook clearly establishes relevance of the study
- ☐ Background provides contextual grounding (not a literature review)
- ☐ Problem statement identifies a genuine, researchable gap
- ☐ Problem is specific, bounded, and defensible
- ☐ Purpose statement is concise and logically derived from the problem
- ☐ Research questions are numbered, aligned, and answerable
- ☐ Significance statement demonstrates both theoretical and practical contribution
- ☐ Key terms are clearly defined and sourced
- ☐ Chapter organization preview is present

II. Scholarly Grounding (Literature Command)

- ☐ Student demonstrates command of foundational literature
- ☐ Recent scholarship is meaningfully integrated
- ☐ Research gap is explicitly articulated
- ☐ Theoretical framework is clearly identified
- ☐ Theoretical framework is justified relative to the problem
- ☐ Framework aligns with research questions

III. Design Alignment (Methodological Coherence)

- ☐ Research design directly addresses research questions
- ☐ Methodology is appropriate to question type
- ☐ Design justification is explicitly articulated
- ☐ Scope is feasible within doctoral timeline
- ☐ Timeline is realistic and defensible

IV. Population & Sampling Integrity

- ☐ Population is clearly defined
- ☐ Sampling strategy is appropriate
- ☐ Inclusion/exclusion criteria are defensible

☐ Sample size rationale is provided
☐ Access feasibility confirmed

V. Data Collection & Instrumentation

☐ Data collection procedures are replicable
☐ Instruments or interview protocols described or included
☐ Measurement approach aligns with research questions
☐ Data management plan described

VI. Data Analysis Alignment

☐ Analysis plan matches data type
☐ Statistical procedures justified (if quantitative)
☐ Coding/thematic process articulated (if qualitative)
☐ Mixed-method integration explained (if applicable)
☐ Validity/reliability or trustworthiness addressed
☐ Limitations acknowledged

VII. Ethical & Compliance Readiness

☐ Ethical risks identified
☐ Informed consent process described
☐ IRB status clarified
☐ Confidentiality procedures defined

Red Flags — Stop and Revise Before Committee Review

☐ Problem statement is broad, vague, or descriptive
☐ No explicit theoretical framework
☐ Methodology does not align with research questions
☐ Scope exceeds doctoral feasibility
☐ Insufficient recent literature engagement
☐ Analysis plan underdeveloped or misaligned
☐ No clear contribution articulated

If any red flag is present, proposal advancement should pause.

Two Weeks Before Defense: Readiness Checklist

☐ Student has circulated final draft to full committee

☐ All committee members confirmed attendance

☐ Defense logistics confirmed (room, technology, format)

☐ Student has prepared 20–30 minute overview presentation

☐ Mock defense conducted with feedback incorporated

☐ Student can articulate study limitations and implications

☐ Student prepared responses to anticipated questions

☐ Committee members submitted preliminary questions/concerns

☐ Student understands post-defense revision process

IRB Application Completeness Checklist

☐ Protocol narrative addresses all required institutional elements

☐ Informed consent form uses approved institutional template

☐ Recruitment materials attached and compliant

☐ Data collection instruments included (surveys, interview guides, etc.)

☐ Data security and storage plan clearly detailed

☐ CITI (or equivalent) training certificates current

☐ Chair/advisor reviewed and approved submission

☐ Research timeline feasible and aligned with study scope

☐ Budget and participant compensation clearly explained (if applicable)

ARB Readiness Checklist

☐ Proposal follows institutional template exactly

☐ Problem–purpose–method alignment is explicit

☐ Literature review demonstrates gap and contribution

☐ Theoretical framework is clearly identified and justified

☐ Methodology is rigorous and appropriate to research questions

☐ All committee members have formally approved the proposal

☐ Student can defend all methodological choices without reliance on notes

Appendix D: AI Usage Frameworks
Reviewing AI-Assisted Student Work

☐ Student disclosed AI tool usage in accordance with institutional policy

☐ AI usage is appropriate for the task (e.g., ideation, outlining, refinement—not wholesale writing)

☐ Student demonstrates clear understanding of any AI-generated or AI-influenced content

☐ Student can explain and defend AI-influenced claims or arguments

☐ Original intellectual contribution is evident throughout the work

☐ All cited sources have been independently verified (no AI-generated or fabricated references)

☐ Writing reflects the student's authentic scholarly voice

☐ Student substantially revised, critiqued, or enhanced any AI-generated output

Red Flags — Pause and Investigate

☐ Sudden and unexplained shift in writing quality or tone

☐ Citation inconsistencies or unverifiable references

☐ Generic, overly polished, or non-contextualized content

☐ Inability to explain methodology, theory, or findings in the student's own words

☐ Resistance to discussing how the work was produced

About the Author

Dr. David A. Schippers, Sc.D., CISSP, is not your typical academic. A scholar-practitioner, systems thinker, and mentor forged in both corporate complexity and educational reform, he brings a rare combination of strategic precision and ethical fire to the heart of doctoral education.

With a doctorate in cybersecurity and years of leadership in higher education, Dr. Schippers has chaired dissertations, redesigned doctoral programs from the ground up, and helped institutions move from stagnation to innovation. As a Chief Academic Officer, former technology/cybersecurity director, and lifelong investigator of both digital systems and human behavior, he's spent his career asking one question:

Why are we still replicating broken models of mentorship—and who benefits from keeping them intact?

The Master Key is not just a guidebook. It is a confrontation with legacy systems that confuse rigor with cruelty, equate silence with scholarship, and reward faculty for hoarding knowledge rather than multiplying it. Dr. Schippers challenges the status quo with unapologetic clarity— while equipping faculty to build new, ethical, high-impact ways of leading students through the most vulnerable phase of their academic journey.

His writing weaves the tactical with the philosophical, blending practical rubrics with ethical introspection, and systems-level reform with personal transformation. He believes chairs are not gatekeepers—they are architects of intellectual becoming. And that belief drives everything in these pages.

Dr. Schippers continues his goal to mentor faculty who are ready to stop perpetuating harm and start unlocking potential and individuate each doctoral mentor to new levels of mastery.

This book is not polite. It's necessary. And so is the kind of mentorship it calls you to become.

Continue the Conversation with Dr. David A. Schippers

If *The Master Key* resonated with you, your journey does not end here.

Dr. David A. Schippers writes at the intersection of leadership, higher education, cybersecurity, and artificial intelligence, challenging conventional thinking while equipping professionals with practical frameworks for real-world impact. His books confront complexity directly, offering clarity where institutions, systems, and leaders often fall short.

Explore other titles by Dr. Schippers:

Burn the Script: Kill the Leadership Theater, Lead for Real
A direct challenge to performative leadership culture. Built from decades of executive and academic experience, this book equips leaders to make difficult decisions, build trust under pressure, and lead with clarity rather than slogans.

The Force of Technology
A comprehensive examination of innovation, cybersecurity, and risk management in a rapidly evolving digital landscape. Designed for leaders and professionals navigating technological disruption with strategic discipline.

The Scholar's Key: Hidden Knowledge for Doctoral Achievement
A structured, principled roadmap for doctoral candidates seeking clarity, momentum, and resilience in advanced academic work.

Across disciplines and industries, Dr. Schippers' work shares a common thread: formation over performance, integrity over appearance, and leadership grounded in responsibility.

Whether you serve in higher education, industry, government, or executive leadership, his books provide frameworks that endure beyond trends and tactics.

To discover more titles, speaking engagements, and academic resources, search for **Dr. David A. Schippers** wherever books are sold.

Lead intentionally. Build wisely. Strengthen what holds everything together.